# *Becoming a* **Religious Sister**

*Eric Erikson and Donald Winnicott in Dialogue*

# Table of Contents

## *Acknowledgments*

My journey as a religious woman in a multicultural and international religious congregation and as a psychoanalyst has been one of hope and courage. It has been a long journey, but my heart is full of gratitude to God for his gift of life and good health through all these years of study and learning to know and deeply appreciate my depth. I want to thank in a special way the admissions team in Graduate Theological Foundation, who accepted me into their program and encouraged me in diverse ways to reach this point in my life.

My thanks go to the sisters, or nuns, who went to the trouble of participating in the research by providing their valuable responses to the questionnaire. This project would not have been possible without your wonderful support of the different religious communities I contacted. My special thanks go to my clients, who gave me the permission to work with them, learn and appreciate them, and use their stories as they became who they were meant to be. I am very grateful.

My immense gratitude goes to my mentor, Rev. Dr. Gordon Edwards, for his support and encouragement to undertake this program. I want to thank you, Dr. Edwards, for your devotion, patience, dedication, and scrutiny to enhance my presentation.

I am equally grateful to Drs. Charles Ignatius and Charles Udokang for reviewing my work and offering constructive criticisms. Thank you for giving me the opportunity to call you at odd times to ask questions.

I would like to express my thanks to my sisters, especially Sisters Faustina Quayson, Faustina Ganaa, Cecelia Bosomtwi, and Lucy Dei, for their encouragement. Sister Faustina, thank you for the arrangement of the tables in the work, and Sister Lucy, thank you for helping me with the data-reduction process.

I also wish to thank Dr. Fredrickson for her support and encouragement. I appreciate my parents, now deceased, who made sure that I went to school at a time when girls' education was not valued much in my culture and who encouraged and supported me throughout the journey of my religious life. Thank you.

# *Abstract*

William James's book The Variety of Religious Experience speaks to the fact that, in every human being, there is an inner desire for something much deeper. He writes, "We hunger and thirst … after righteousness," "We find the Lord in a sweet savor," and "We taste and see that he is good" (2009, 17). This is the same desire that speaks to the hearts of those who choose to enter a religious life or life of ministry. James quotes St. Francis de Sales in his description of the "horizon of quietude,"—specifically, "In this state the soul is like a child at the breast, whose mother cares for him whilst he is still in her arms, makes her milk distill into his mouth without him even moving his lips" (2009, 17). This quotation reminds me of Winnicott's idea of good-enough mothering, which means that the ordinary, normal preoccupations of the mother help shape the growing child's sense of identity (Winnicott 1986). The divine in each human, which may mean different things to different people, brings an "awe-ness" in the presence of God, which Otto Rudolf talks about in his book *The Idea of the Holy* (2010, 12–15). The awe-ness feeling can also be compared to Winnicott's idea of capacity to believe—that is, the concept of "believing in" must be present in the child's growing-up process so that, when the child grows up, there is a place to believe in God (1990, 93). Winnicott adds that, when a child does not develop this capacity to believe, she finds it difficult to accept moral education in adult life (93). (Because we are discussing this in terms of nuns or religions sisters, we use the female pronouns she and her.) The capacity to believe will provide a pathway and easy access for the person choosing to enter a religious life or become a nun or religious sister. This capacity to believe explored by Winnicott is akin to the basic trust Erikson portrayed in the first of his eight stages of development with their appropriate basic strength (Erikson, 1950, 1963). According to Erikson, if the child realizes that the mother is consistent in her caregiving, the child begins to learn basic trust (1994). However, the child learns basic mistrust if she finds no correspondence between her needs and the environment. This lack has repercussions in adulthood. It is the beginning of a journey toward psychological imbalance or disturbance.

This study was undertaken to fully understand the extent of the psychological imbalance or immaturity of the individuals answering the call to the religious life. Researchers have focused solely on religious life and not on the chaotic behaviors that prevail in these religious communities.

The survey method employed in this study was simple random sampling. This method was determined to be appropriate because it enabled the subjects of the study to be themselves and not be manipulated in the process. In other words, this research is not experimental. Sampling was conducted to access a representative segment of the general population from which information on the entire population could be inferred. In all, 200 respondents of sisters from 5 different religious groups were surveyed using a questionnaire and a group process to fill in the information. The first part of the questionnaire contained 16 items and was designed to explore respondents' experiences with their fathers while growing up. The second part of the questionnaire listed 59 behaviors in 6 columns, and respondents were to tick off behavior that they had observed in their congregations, in finally professed sisters, in temporally professed sisters, novices, postulants, and themselves. The study's finding was that the listed behaviors are all prevalent in the various religious communities and in both people who grew up with their fathers in the home and those who did not. They all have major anxiety issues, trust issues, untrusting issues, and an inability to handle crises, to mention just a few. Based on the findings, it is recommended that all sisters, including superiors and leaders, explore their childhood upbringing to identify how the lack of nurturing and emotional support from parents or primary/significant caregivers has impacted their lives. A recommendation was issued that basic psychological courses be taught to current sisters as well as those wishing to join the various congregations so they can self-evaluate and see whether or not they fit this type of life. In this way, the chaotic ways of relating to one another will be limited, and people will find contentment in the lives they have chosen.

# Chapter 1

# Background of the Study

The background of the study focused on digging deeper into the driving forces behind people's choosing a way of life that is dedicated to a lifetime of ministry. This means that, while choosing a spiritual path, certain psychological components play a vital role in the maturation process of young adults who are ready to choose this way of life—this vocation, call to a religious life, or call to the priesthood.

Walton explains that administration is an activity concerned with directing the activities of people working within an organization in their reciprocal relation to the end that the organizational purpose may be attained (1969). While a business administrator's goal is geared toward increase in productivity, the goal of a religious leader is to foster unity and peace to enhance the members' lives. To achieve this goal, the administrator or leader must involve himself or herself with making right choices and decisions to ensure that the individuals in religious life play their respective roles in a satisfying manner. Thus, the effectiveness and growth of a religious institution depends, to a large extent, on its leaders because, if the center cannot hold, everything will fall apart (Achebe 1996).

Human activities have always fascinated me. I often wondered while growing up about the way people related to one another, especially when it came to the words they used and the specific behaviors they manifested. I am thinking of a range from abusive words thrown at one another to violent acts, such as physical fighting and so forth. I remember asking my mother one day, "Where do people learn these behaviors?" With no satisfying answer given, I have tried in my own way to search for answers and to understand people's ways of thinking and reasoning. From my observation and experience of working with children and adults, I have found that many of the behaviors, whether good or bad, spring from the way people were taught in their childhoods, both by their parents and by teachers in the school. Much depends on the way they grew up as adolescents and the way they were nurtured, supported, and guided by others around them. Once these individuals become adults, they begin to think seriously about a career and a life that will satisfy their visions and bring happiness. They realize that they can choose a way of life. One such choice is for a person to become a nun or religious sister. This is what we call a religious vocation, a call from God. The person hears the call and freely chooses to accept it. This call is an invitation to this individual, who wholeheartedly chooses to love God and neighbor. Diverse individuals choose to answer God's calls. According to Hamman, "There is the fierce and fiery Moses; the courageous Joshua; ... the stubborn, whining Jonah; the self-confident and resilient Paul; ... the faint-hearted, yet foundational Peter" (2014, 13). These individuals from the Old and the New Testaments in their own capacity answered their calls to love God and neighbor, bringing that call into the spaces of who they were. Similarly, one can ask, "Who is this person interiorly who has freely chosen this life of dedication, and what does this individual bring to this ministry?"

Having had the privilege of being a nun or religious sister myself and living in other parts of the world with other religious sisters ministering to communities, I have witnessed so many behaviors of individuals—some positive and some not so positive, even from talented men and women called to ministry. The ones whose thinking and behaviors were not positive have brought many heartaches and sorrows to others. As experience tells us, leaders or superiors cannot be happy and effective when there are too many disturbances within the communities; poor interpersonal relationships between them and the sisters will result in conflicts, mental agony, and poor moral standards. Similarly, individual sisters cannot utilize their prayer time, studies, and activities properly and efficiently if there is lack of peace and harmony in the environment in which they live and call home, to which the religious person can return after her apostolic labors. To effect a possible change, all must be enlightened to look within themselves and the system and find the causes of and remedies for dysfunctional behaviors.

Much has been said and written about religious vocations and religious life in general. Many articles and books about how to attract young men and women into this life have emerged. Many young people, both men and women, have asked themselves if they have a vocation or a call to this kind of life. Even with all these questions and lack of clarity, many men and women over the years have felt called to religious life—to become a nun, religious sister, or religious priest—and they have responded. It is a life that some have found fulfillment in, while others have not. Many have left, and others have stayed for fear of not knowing what else to do if they leave. Some have been asked to leave by their leaders; others have left on their own. It is a life that still attracts people all over the world. Some countries hardly attract people to join, some countries to a lesser extent, and others, especially some African countries, still attract young men and women, probably because this way of life is relatively new. In this study, I will focus on women who choose a religious way of life and the psychological maturity that is required in their choices.

**Statement of the Problem**

Although the religious life continues to attract some young people, there has been an increase in poor leadership, ineffective decision-making, and members' behavioral problems, such as slander, favoritism, quarreling among themselves or with others, in-fighting, and arbitrarily sending home younger members. These problems have contributed to the unpleasant experiences of these young individuals. For young men and women to feel attracted to this life and continue to feel fulfilled, it is necessary to understand the psychological inner life of each person making the choice. Most importantly, the person making the choice should be helped to understand his or her inner life. This person eventually will become a leader and make decisions for others. If change is to occur, we need to look at each person who makes this choice through a psychological lens. The study will take into consideration how our history as people and our past life experiences influence the choices we make. The study will also focus on how a young woman's inner life contributes to her outward activities. The choice of such a life implies a psychological maturity combined with a vision of what one wants in life. Every individual marches toward adulthood with physical, psychological, and social growth. Therefore, it will be important to know what should be done, if anything, to enable a person to become a good and mature nun or religious sister. Erik Erikson, in his book Childhood and Society (1950, 1963), made us aware that we as persons are influenced greatly by the families and societies that welcomed us into the world. How much then is a person's inner life a contributing factor to her outward activities?

**Purpose and Significance of the Study**

My interest is to look critically at what a person, particularly a young girl, who has chosen to respond to the call of God brings to the religious life. The focus is on finding out what comprises the identity of a religious sister. The study will also analyze the interactions among individuals in religious communities and the ways these interactions affect the individuals, whether positively or negatively. I have been a nun or religious sister for more than thirty years and have experienced all the difficult phases this life offers. I have had the opportunity to interact with my own religious community and with other nuns or religious sisters in other communities around the world, and I now interact with them as a licensed psychoanalyst, a fact which has made it more compelling to undertake this study.

With my new identity, this study would give me an opportunity to develop in-depth knowledge about the problem in existence. It would allow young men and women contemplating the religious life, those who are already living the life and facing challenges, and those in leadership positions to understand the implication of the problem. This study will broaden the minds of young people who desire the religious life and help them to prepare themselves psychologically when making the decision. It will further provide a construct for use in screening young people who choose to embrace this life. Women who choose this way of life will be empowered to be who they were meant to be and live a fuller life in all circumstances. Rollo May put this beautifully: "Our aim is to discover ways in which we can stand against the insecurities of our time, to find a center of strength with ourselves; and as far as we can, to point the way toward achieving values and goals which can be depended upon in a day when very little is secure" (1981, viii).

**Scope of the Study**

Issues related to decision-making in religious life are vast. In this study, I will focus on what characterizes a person as authentically religious. What will be the psychological profile of a mature religious sister or nun? I will touch on basic religious life. The findings of this study will be applicable to other nuns or religious sisters and communities experiencing the same issue. However, the focus of this study will be the psychological makeup of a sister or nun, primarily accessing the developmental theory of Erik Erikson's eight psychosocial stages and Donald Winnicott's six capacities. Erikson and Winnicott will be engaged in dialogue with each other.

Although Winnicott and Erikson's theoretical frame will be engaged, this study will not be driven by nor beholden to only what Erikson or Winnicott has to say on every point. The study is not intended to further explain what Erikson or Winnicott has to say, and the researcher will not attempt to reconcile differences between them. Both theorists will be engaged in dialogue with the researcher's concept of what makes for a good nun or religious sister, whose mental and emotional development are really the focus of this study.

**Limitations of the Study**

During the research study, some sisters offered resistance and a lack of support. Many felt this issue is as old as life itself and their honest responses might make their leaders look upon them as not having genuine vocation. Others intimated that they would put their vocation at risk if they voiced their opinions out loud, and still others felt that engaging in this study would be interpreted as a breach of their vow of obedience. Older religious sisters complained that they have no time to provide the needed information. One congregation did not allow any of her members to respond to the questionnaire for fear that the questionnaire might foment "unwanted" questions. This lack of interest and support from the sisters (nuns) put a limitation on the extent to which the findings of this study could be appropriately generalized. In addition, other aspects of religious life got in the way of this study—for instance, some felt that everything that happens to a religious community can be spiritualized, thus robbing the same of its psychological significance. The emphasized role of the Holy Spirit within the religious communities caused others to play down the psychological significance of this study among some of the sisters (nuns).

## Definition of Terms

Here are some important terms that might need clarification.

## Aspirancy or candidacy:

An aspirant or a candidate is one who is making the first step to contemplate becoming a religious sister or nun. In the process of making the decision, one is called a candidate or aspirant, meaning that this individual is aspiring to become a religious sister, brother, or nun. This period has no time limit.

## Catechumen:

These are adults seeking to be initiated or received into the Catholic Church. They go through a period of preparation for three years in which they learn about the Catholic Church and the scriptures, after which they receive Baptism, Confirmation, and the Holy Eucharist, also called Holy Communion.

## Consecrated life:

This is defined by the Catholic Church as a stable form of Christian living by faithful people who are called to follow Christ in a more exacting way recognized by the church (section 573, para. 1 of the Code of Canon Law, 1983). Consecrated life, when it is used specifically, refers to men and women who have professed the evangelical counsels (poverty, chastity, and obedience) in their various institutes and pledge to follow Christ more closely. They are set apart for Christ and dedicated to the service of the Church. A diocesan bishop consecrates them according to the approved liturgical rite (Vocation Centre 2021).

**Diocesan Bishop:**

The Catholic Church has different dioceses or areas of jurisdiction of which bishops are in charge. A bishop or archbishop has a pastoral charge of a diocese or archdiocese. In the Catholic Church, the bishop is entrusted with pastoral care of a local church (diocese) over which he holds jurisdiction. He is responsible for teaching, governing, and sanctifying the faithful of the diocese. And religious sisters are part of the faithful (Wikipedia 2021).

**Diocesan Rights:**

The religious congregations erected by bishops that have not obtained a decree of approval from the Holy See (canon 589, 1917, 1983) are diocesan rights. They serve mostly the people the diocese (Wikipedia 2021 c).

**Final Professed:**

This is the stage in which the sister makes her final commitment to God and the Church. The person now is known as a finally professed sister. Usually, the sister is given a ring as a sign of her total dedication to God and the Church.

**Novitiate:**

This is the third stage, at which the individual is called a novice. Novitiate means "in training," or learning about the chosen congregation and its rules and customs. The atmosphere and routine are much more rigorous than those of the postulants.

**PC, Perfectae Caritatis:**

(English is "Perfect Charity"). This is the decree on the adaptation and renewal of the religious life. It is an encyclical (letter) proclaimed by His Holiness Pope Paul VI, on October 26, 1965 (Holy See 2021).

**Pontifical rights:**

Religious congregations erected or approved by the Holy See are pontifical rights. They are directly under the authority of the Holy See (section 589 of the Code of Canon Law, 1983; Wikipedia 2021e).

**Postulancy:**

This is the second stage after the individual has decided on the particular society or congregation she wishes to join. The person is now called a postulant for a period from six months to two years, depending on the congregation and society (Wikipedia 2022 f).

**Religious Vows:**

These are public vows made by members of religious communities, according to their practices. In the Catholic Church, the vows are called evangelical counsels, and they are poverty, chastity, and obedience (Wikipedia 2021f).

**Rosary Beads:**

Beads on a rosary represent sets of prayers used by the Catholic Church. The prayers are composed of the Lord's Prayer and the Hail Mary (Dummies.com 2021g).

**SOS:**

This is an international morse-code distress signal, known worldwide. It has been known to mean "save our ship" and "save our souls.: It is a distress call. For my purpose it is a call or signal for help (Wikipedia 2021h).

**Temporal Professed:**

After two years in the novitiate, the sister makes a public profession of vows and renews for six consecutive years. At this stage, the sister continues to learn and grow in her understanding of, as well as her relationship with, God. It is called temporal because the commitment made is not final (Wikipedia 2021i).

**Organization of the Study**

The study is divided into six chapters.

**Chapter 1** deals with the following: background of the study, statement of the problem, purpose or significance of the study, scope, limitation of the study, definitions of terms, and the organization of the study.

**Chapter 2** is devoted to the review of literature related to the topic under study. It deals with the basic concept of a human, basic religious life experiences, and the inner life of the individual embarking on this psychological journey. We will review Donald W. Winnicott's six capacities and Erik Erikson's developmental stages as these relate to a healthy or an unhealthy personality of the individual. We will also discuss development in terms of Bowlby and Ainsworth's attachment theories.

**Chapter 3** deals with the description of the research methods and design, sampling and sampling techniques, population, development of the consistency of the instruments, pilot study, data collection and analysis, the questionnaire for interviews, and the research hypothesis.

**Chapter 4** addresses the data analysis as per the findings. Tables will be presented and engaged directly.

**Chapter 5** comprises the summary of findings and discussions.

**Chapter 6** deals with the overview of the work. There will be a brief **Conclusions** section to close out the study.

Finally, an **Appendix** and the **Bibliography** will be presented at the end of the study.

*Chapter 2*

# Related Literature Review

The review is meant to aid the researcher in identifying methods, measures, and approaches used in earlier research to obtain information concerning the topic under study. It is intended to present a picture of the inner life of a young girl who has chosen to embark upon this journey of answering God's call as she interacts with her surroundings and expresses herself in normal and not-so-normal behavior. From this inner life arise things that are mainly responsible for what a person says or does. Psychoanalysis has taught us that the infant has many desires as the ego develops into personhood. Carl Jung believed that each person possessed an inherited tendency to move toward growth, perfection, and completion, and he called this innate disposition the self. Maslow believed that an individual can integrate well enough in physical, social, intellectual, emotional and spiritual needs if they can have a full use of their talents, potentials and capacities. He calls this self-actualization (1970, 1971). We need to have some basic understanding of the person and her personality.

**The Nun or Religious Sister as a Person**

A religious sister is one who has chosen to follow Christ and to be poor, chaste, and obedient. She is one who has chosen to participate in the church's mission in the service of the poor, the sick or homebound, youth or parish religious programs, and so on. She has decided to have a deep desire to observe the evangelical counsels as a commandment and to spend time with Jesus. Most importantly, she has emotional balance—that is, the ability to be aware of and recognize her emotions as they occur and how they impacts her daily life and to know how to work through them successfully.

Rollo May states, "To undertake this 'venture of becoming aware of ourselves' and to discover the source of inner strength and security which are the rewards of such venture, let us start at the beginning by asking, what is this person?" (1981, 57) The concept of a person can be very challenging to define. The word is often used as synonym for human being. The adverse of the Diagnostic and Statistical Manual of Mental Disorders (American Psychiatric Association 2013) is true: a healthy person results from the enduring pattern of inner experience and behavior that cohere markedly with the expectations of the individual's culture; this pattern is manifested in the areas of cognitive, affectivity, interpersonal functioning, and impulsive control.

**Definition of a Person**

The American Heritage College Dictionary defines person as "the composite of characteristics that make up an individual's personality, the self" (1993, 1,019). In Rollo May's book Man's Search for Himself, he adds, "Consciousness of self, this capacity to see oneself as though from the outside, is the distinctive characteristic of man" (1981, 58). He goes on to say, "This capacity for consciousness of ourselves gives us the ability to see ourselves as others see us and to have empathy with others. It underlines our remarkable capacity to transport ourselves" (58).

Gary L. Harbaugh, in his book Pastor as Person: Maintaining Personal Integrity in the Choices and Challenges of Ministry, views a person in terms of wholeness—that is, body, mind, emotions, and soul. He defines wholeness thusly: "From a secular perspective wholeness means thinking about persons as physical, mental, emotional and social being" (1984, 21). To be able to understand what makes a person count as a person we ought to consider the personal identity of this individual.

**Definition of Personality**

As it is difficult to define what a person is, so it is with personality. Personality theorists have proposed different meanings because they do not agree on one definition. This is because each theorist approached the subject from his or her own perspective. Freud offered a personality theory that has enabled another theorist to follow suit. Cameron quoted from Freud's 1925 biography: "Looking back then, over the patchwork of my life's labors, I can say that I have made many beginnings and thrown out many suggestions. Something will come out of them in the future, though I cannot tell myself whether it will be much or little. I can, however, express a hope that I have opened up a pathway for an important advance in our knowledge" (1963, viii). This pathway left by Freud has led other theorists to look critically at what goes on in the inner world of the individual. Gordon Allport states, "Personality includes a wide variety of adjustive activities, characteristics of the person and rendering the human organism the unique unit that it is" (1955, 61). He added, "At birth we start with an organism (or individual) which develops unique modes of adjusting to and mastering the environment; these modes constitute personality" (61).

Allport later adjusted his definition to read, "Personality is the dynamic organization with the individual of those psychophysical systems that determine his characteristics, behavior and thought" (1961, 28). This view emphasizes the uniqueness of the individual and the internal cognition and motivational processes that influence behavior. Personality development to Norman "is a gradual transformation from biological organism to biosocial person. Each child through continual interactions with other human beings, in human environment, comes in time to think, to feel, and to act fundamentally as others feel and act" (1963, p. 26). According to Feist and Feist, "Personality is a pattern of relatively permanent traits and individuality to a person's behavior" (2009, 4). They explain that "traits contribute to individual differences in behavior, consistency of behavior over time, and stability of behavior across situation. Traits may be unique but their pattern is different for each individual" (Feist and Feist 2009, 4).

Behavior is determined by relatively stable traits that are the fundamental units of one's personality. Traits predispose one to act in a certain way, regardless of the situation. This means that traits should remain consistent across situations and over time but may vary among individuals. This goes to establish the fact that everyone has his or her own traits and therefore own personalities. So, then, a young woman who chooses to become a religious sister (nun) must have her own traits, personality, and identity. One of the theorists concerned about person, personality, and identity is Erik Erikson.

Erikson (1902-1994) was born to Danish parents near Frankfurt. His mother came from a prominent, cosmopolitan family of Jewish merchants in Copenhagen. She named him Erik Salmonsen. He was born into a single-parent family, and Erikson's mother was unable to let him know who his father was. In his quest to seek his identity, he coined the term identity crisis because going through his own identity crisis became a turning point in his life.

In 1950, Erikson published Childhood and Society, presenting his epigenic life cycle that he called the Eight Ages of Man. It was a cultural supplement to the psychosexual development model. This publication brought Erikson immediate acclaim. In his theory of development, Erikson combined his lifelong interest in psychoanalysis, children, normal human development, and the influence of society in the formation of an individual's psychology. Even though Erikson built upon a Freudian edifice, in contrast he emphasized strength over weakness, health over neurosis, and the future over the past. Erikson proposed an organismic model grounded in an epigenetic, psychosexual, and psychosocial matrix. For Erikson, epigenesis refers to the process through which a succession of potentialities, each having its time of ascendency in hierarchical fashion, builds upon prior ones to assemble the biological and psychological structure of the person (1959, 1980).

Erikson maintained that personality develops in a predetermined order through eight stages of psychosocial development from infancy to adulthood. In each of these stages, the individual experiences a psychosocial crisis that could have either a positive or a negative outcome for the that person's personality development (1980, on health and growth). For Winnicott, the good-enough mothering of the child and the ordinary preoccupation of the mother will form a process of development that is personal and real (1960). The true self is the instinctive core of the personality, and the mother is the total basis of the development of the infant.

**Identity of the Individual**

Identity is a fact of being who or what a person is. By *identity,* we mean "an individual's sense of self defined by a set of physical and psychological characteristics that is not wholly shared with other person" (*APA Dictionary of Psychology 2006, 463).* It goes on further to say that "it is the awareness that this individual remains the same even though there may be changes" (463). To buttress this point, *The American Heritage College Dictionary* uses four different approaches to defining identity.

The first approach sees identity as "the set of characteristics by which a thing is recognized or known." The second approach sees identity as "set of behavioral or personal traits by which an individual is recognizable as a member of a group," while the third defines it as "the quality or condition of being the same as something else." The fourth is the "distinct personality of an individual regarded as a persisting entity; individuality" (2006, p. 674).

According to their Textbook of Psychoanalysis, Person et al. state that "identity is the enduring experience of the self as a unique, coherent, and relatively consistent entity over time" (2005, 552). Akhtar wrote in Comprehensive Dictionary of Psychoanalysis that the term identity of Psychoanalysis that the term identity was introduced into psychoanalysis by Victor Tausk (1919), who examined how a child discovers itself and asserted that man, throughout life, constantly finds and experiences himself anew (Akhtar 2009, 139). Akhtar added that, currently, a well- established identity consists of seven components:

1. A sustained feeling of self-sameness displaying roughly similar character traits to varied others

2. Temporal continuity in the self- experience

3. Genuineness and authenticity

4. A realistic body image

5. A sense of inner solidity and the associated capacity for peaceful solitude

6. Subjective clarity regarding one's gender

7. An inner solidarity with an ethnic group's ideals and a well-internalized conscience (140)

Erikson, the developmental psychologist, used this concept in his work. He believed that the formation of identity was one of the most important parts of a person's growth processes. His work was associated with the development of the ego in what is known as ego psychology. He believed that the ego develops throughout the various stages of life, that is, a step-by-step growth. This is what is called the epigenetic principle. "Epigenesis means that one characteristic develops on top of another in space and time" (Evans 1967, 21-22) In all these stages, the individual confronts a task, masters it, and then faces new challenges. The stages of development have their appropriate strengths and crises.

- Basic trust has its opposite side of basic mistrust. The inevitable clash between the basic trust and basic mistrust is the first crisis of the infant. If it is resolved successfully, the result is hope, the basic strength of the infant.
- The next stage is early childhood. The task is autonomy, and its opposite is shame and doubt. When it is resolved, the result is will, which becomes the basic strength in the early childhood.
- Next is the play age. The task is initiative, and its opposite is guilt. If it is successfully resolved, the result for the child will have purpose at this play-age period.
- The next stage is the school age, in which the task is industry and its opposite inferiority. If this is successfully resolved, the school-age child has competency as the basic strength.
- The next stage is the adolescence phase. The task is identity, and its opposite is identity confusion. When the adolescent can resolve the crisis, the result will be fidelity, the basic strength of adolescence.

- The next stage is young adulthood. The task is intimacy, and the opposite is isolation. When resolved, the basic strength at this stage will be love.
- The next stage is adulthood, in which the task is generativity and its opposite stagnation. When resolved, the basic strength at this stage will be care.
- The last stage is old age, with a task of ego integrity and its opposite is despair. When resolved, the basic strength is wisdom. (Erikson 1980, 57-105)

Each phase not successfully completed results in a "core pathology" (Feist and Feist 2009, 24).

The eight stages are most often presented with the syntonic quotient mentioned first, followed by the dystonic element—that is, trust vs. mistrust, autonomy vs. shame and doubt. The syntonic (harmonious) element supports growth and expansion, offers goals, and celebrates self-respect and commitment of the very finest. Dystonic (disruptive) elements often confront and challenge us. We should recognize that circumstances may place the dystonic in a more dominant position. Erikson reviews stage by stage what the aged individual faces in terms of the syntonic and dystonic elements and the tensions with which she must cope.

In an article, Kendra Cherry explains that one of the main elements of Erikson's psychosocial stage theory is the development of ego identity. It is a conscious sense of the self that we develop through social interactions and that is constantly changing due to new experiences and the information we acquire in our daily interactions with others.

Donald W. Winnicott (1896-1971), a British pediatrician, psychiatrist, sociologist, and psychoanalyst, was well known for his concepts of the holding environment, good-enough mothering, true and false selves, and transitional objects. The mother-infant theory describes the process of developing oneself as one grows in relations to others in the environment. These relationships are formed during the early interactive years between an infant and her primary caregivers (Winnicott 1962, pp. 56-72). In Winnicott's six capacities, one can grow to be a more secure individual and more compassionate because these capacities can be nurtured and cultivated. We can find ways to be less destructive to others and to ourselves. We can choose to nurture these capacities when we recognize that we have some that are underdeveloped. In these capacities, the infant and the mother's bond is the key to healthy development, which is rooted in relationships and micro-interactions with other people. Winnicott focuses on transitional objects for comfort and not-me identification: the good-enough mothering (1982). His developmental stages were unity, transition, and interdependence. Winnicott believed that his three developmental stages could be met only when the good-enough mother plays her role well. Let's consider Winnicott's three developmental stages.

**Unity:** First, the child needs an illusion of being connected with and not separated from the mother. If things go well, the child feels omnipotent and in complete control of the mother, the feeling it gets when the mother responds to the baby's needs. During this stage, the child feels connected with the mother and becomes independent slowly. When the child is held by the mother and rocked or caressed to sleep, the child gradually learns to fall asleep when she is put down. Similarly, when a mother responds to a child's cry of hunger without an angry outburst, the child learns trust.

**Transition:** Transition is the second stage of Winnicott's three developmental stages. This is the stage where disillusionment takes place. The child recognizes both her own separateness and that of her parents, that they also have lives to live and must be considered. The disconnection and removal of the illusion, when done suddenly, can be very traumatic and shocking for the child, so this needs to occur as gently as possible. When this stage is done successfully, it will strengthen the ego rather than damage it. By removing the illusion from the child in well-timed, small doses, the good-enough mother helps develop a healthy sense of independence in the child. The child uses a transitional object as its substitute for the mother. In the transitional stage, the mother is not always there for the child, but the child learns to be more independent. When a baby falls asleep while the mother is holding her or him, the baby slowly and gradually learns that she needs to fall asleep when put down by the mother.

**Interdependence:** During this third stage, the child develops a healthy false self that can be presented to the world and with which she is comfortable. But total independence is not possible because we all are dependent on someone. There is more independence because the child now is able to play with others without the mother being at her side. The job of the good-enough mother is to guide the child through these stages by providing early connections and gradual release (Winnicott 1960, 83-88).

The object-relationship school of thought focused on early childhood, primarily the first three or four years of life. It is a theory of human personality developed from the study of the therapist-client relationship as it reflects the mother-infant duo. The theory holds that the infant's experience in relationship with the mother or the caregiver is the primary determinant of personality formation. The "object" of the theory is not to be confused with a toy or subject of affection but focuses on internal objects. The breast that feeds the hungry infant is the good breast, while the hungry infant who finds no breast is in relation to the "bad" object. Object-relationship theory also holds that, when the needs of the child are not met by the parents, a pathological turning away from reality takes place (Fairbairn 1992). Winnicott recognized that we are not driven by instincts but that we search for and are shaped by our early relationships. He observed in infants the gradual formation of the self, a self that can have an experience that is real. In his six capacities, individuals must develop and possess, maintain, and enjoy healthy relationships with themselves, with others, and with the world.

For Winnicott, these capacities can be cultivated irrespective of our age. "Capacities speak to certain innate abilities all persons possess to some extent.... A tension we experience around capacities is that they are never achieved" (Hamman 2014, 210).

**The Six Capacities of Donald Winnicott**

Following are descriptions of the six capacities established by Winnicott.

**1.The Capacity to Believe**

This is the ability to be self-confident. It describes a person with inner security. Winnicott's capacity to believe is the ability to trust in others. Trust eludes many people because of their sense of insecurities. We choose to protect ourselves rather than let people know who we are, but often others see through us, and so sometimes we project a false sense of security to cover up. At the emotional stage of life in which the mother is the primary caregiver, she becomes preoccupied with the infant and the father supporting the mother, and the mother identifies with the infant and intuitively knows her infant's needs." This is when trust begins. The mother does not let the infant down; she teaches the child that the mother will always meet the child's needs. The mother learns at this initial stage the different cues of her child, especially the way the child cries so she can tell if the child wants food or warmth or is afraid. If a mother is able to give herself to her infant in this predictable and consistent manner, the mother becomes a good-enough mother, which reassures the infant to go on "being." By making her breast available at the right moment, the mother enables the infant to believe that she has created a small world out of her own need. Sometimes a mother is unable to meet all of the infant's needs, and so the infant feels deprived. When the infant cries and finds no breast to relieve her hunger, there is a delay. The delay that exists between the child's expressing a need and having that need met introduces the move toward relative independence as the infant adapts to the new reality. Winnicott believes this is good because, through this, the infant can learn how to wait to be fed and will also learn to tolerate waiting period. For Winnicott, a mother who is "too good" always anticipates the infant's needs and provides it, and this is as harmful as the mother who neglects the infant's needs.

Winnicott agrees that, as the emotional and relational needs of the infant are taken care of or met, the child tries to widen her social circles, thus striving toward independence (1990).

Winnicott reminds us that a child's self develops in a "holding/facilitating" environment where the child is held appropriately and adequately and where external anxieties do not impinge on the child. In some families, growing children learn early enough to care for themselves if their emotional and physical needs are not met. Let us think of a child who grows up with drunken parents, a child who is sexually molested and told it is her fault, or a child who grows up around depressed adults and needs to cheer them up all the time. Think of a child who is expected to be perfect and so does everything expected of her.

Sometimes, when parents' divorce, a child may become, in essence, the mother or father of the home (Winnicott et al. 1986). Such children survive by developing a false self, and as Winnicott puts it, "A false self is always compliant" (1986, 68). Instead of the caregiver's becoming attuned to the child's needs, the child becomes attuned to the needs of the caregiver. When the primary caregiver or mother is unable to protect the infant from undue anxiety, the true self diminishes, and the false self takes over. In other words, the capacity to believe suffers if our true selves are threatened. The capacity to believe, therefore, requires a facilitating or a holding environment—a loving, nurturing, caring human relationship so that the one with the capacity to believe will be comfortable with ambivalence and can carry any uncertainties (Winnicott 1990, 105). Lacking the capacity to believe causes anxiety to a person, especially if this person is unable to hear and hold the difficult life story of another person.

## 2. The Capacity to Be Alone

This describes the ability for an individual to contain her emotions and be able to relate with others (Winnicott). This capacity is the most important sign of maturity in emotional development. The basis of this capacity to be alone is the experience of being alone in the presence of another. An infant with a weak ego organization may be alone because of reliable ego support from her mother or primary caregiver. This capacity to be alone needs a reliable presence of a good-enough mother or caregiver. Winnicott believes that this capacity to be alone is linked to self-discovery and transformation of self, and as such it is achievable. Winnicott was a close observer of children during his practice. He observed that from the age of one and a half to two years, children begin to play alone.

The good-enough mother creates a reliable environment for the child and also remains present in the child's mind even if she steps out for a few seconds. The child believes the mother is present. It is interesting to note that, when a child is playing in the presence of the mother or caregiver, the child leaves the play activity, runs to the mother or caregiver for a period, and then returns and reengages in the play activity. Seeking out an adult means the child might have encountered some emotional challenge in the course of play and so needed adult support before returning to play alone again. This child is slowly learning how to access, deal with, and contain emotions. Winnicott referred to this seeking out of the adult during the play time as "seeking ego-relatedness." This refers to the" relationship between two people, one of whom at any rate is alone; perhaps both are alone, yet the presence of each is important to the other" (Winnicott 1958, 30). When the child is in the presence of the adult, the togetherness is physical at first, and then the images of the loved one become internalized. Winnicott is certain that children internalize good objects or images. For him, "being alone in the presence of someone can take place at a very early stage, when the ego immaturity is naturally balanced by ego-support from the mother. In the course of time the individual introjects the ego-supportive mother and in this way becomes able to be alone without frequent references to the mother or mother symbol" (32). Unfortunately, we internalize bad objects as well, including mothers or parents whose punitive or persecutory nature haunts us (scolds or criticizes) all the time.

If one achieves the capacity to be alone in the presence of others, this suggests that the individual grew up in a caring, holding environment and is able to live creatively in the world as well as able to contain the tension that living with others brings. "The individual who has developed the capacity to be alone is constantly able to rediscover the personal impulse, and the personal impulse is not wasted because being alone is something which (though paradoxically) always implies that someone else is there" (Winnicott 1958, 34). So this capacity is related to emotional and spiritual maturity. It creates space for our existence, and when we create space for ourselves, we can then create space for others to live and discover what it means to live in turn.

### 3. The Capacity to Imagine

This describes the ability for an individual to be creative, imaginative, hopeful, and inspirational. It is an ability to come up with mental images of something that is not real or with new and creative ideas. Imagination allows one to explore the past and to imagine the future. It is a tool for recreating one's life, and it plays an important role in our mental health. Winnicott reminds us that the capacity to imagine can only come about if one has a secure sense of being, that is, the capacity to believe. Without the capacity to believe, imagining could be very terrifying experience. To be able to engage the outside world requires the capacity to imagine— the ability to perceive reality even when it is yet to be realized. Just imagine a leader of a religious community who cannot imagine or a group of nuns or sisters who are unable to engage the outside world. The task of leadership requires imagination. If one has the capacity to imagine, one can create, reason, speculate, learn, inspire, think, understand, and do a whole lot of other things. A person who is unable to imagine may be out of touch with the subjective world. Such people have no depth. They cannot come alive. If in a religious community a leader cannot come alive or imagine, the atmosphere becomes dead. But if the leader is one who has imagination and can create or encourage others to imagine, then their community will be vibrant. Winnicott believes that the capacity to imagine has its beginning with the infant who imagines that the breast is its creation, that the infant has created the breast that nurses her. When the baby is hungry and cries and the mother places the breast at the baby's disposal, the infant believes she created it even though the breast has been there all along. This is the child's illusion of omnipotence, of course, which is fitting for that stage of the infant's growth.

To imagine is to live creatively. For Winnicott, living creatively means feeling alive and having meaning, living a life that is not merely reactive but being who you are, not always being who others ask you to be or who you think you need to be so others can love you, as happens all the time in the religious houses. Winnicott says we need no special talent for creative living, and everyone, irrespective of age and physical health, can live creatively. An example of a person's story told during the group process brought home the idea of the true self diminishing when it is threatened and the "killing" of the imaginative mind. (Refer to chapter 6, Overview of the Work.)

## 4. The Capacity to Play

This capacity describes an individual who can be spontaneous and engage others creatively. Play is used in all forms of communication by both adults and children. Most people play creatively even in their conversations. Winnicott recognizes the potential of play as work that children have to do to become adults. Winnicott believes that creative playing facilitates mental growth, and so it is a healthy thing to do. He believes that creativity starts with the infant's first moves to separate herself physically and psychologically from the mother. Through these moves, the baby uses the physical space between herself and the mother to create a world of her own. The infant's creation is what Winnicott calls transitional space. The child uses transitional objects as a mother substitute, such as a teddy bear or a blanket, and treats the objects as she likes (Winnicott 1982). The child develops a new way to play—that is, learning to play alone but in the presence of someone, a responsible adult. This is where the child develops the capacity to be alone. For Winnicott, playing has specific space (1982). It is an experience that occurs in a potential space between mother and baby, and it is in this space where Winnicott believes we become alive.

*Potential space* is a term Winnicott uses to describe good parenting, creativity, and aliveness. We may associate the potential space with love. He states, "Potential space happens only in relation to a feeling of confidence on the part of the baby, that is, confidence related to the dependability of the mother figure or environmental elements, confidence being the evidence of dependability that is being introjected" (Winnicott 1982, 135). In Winnicott's Playing and Reality he adds, "The potential space between the baby and mother, between child and family, between individual and society or the world, depends on experience which leads to trust. It can be looked upon as sacred to the individual in that it is here that the individual experiences creative living" (2005). One experiences love in the potential space. In the potential space, the infant learns how to manipulate objects and discover the limitations of personal power and skills, and that is probably the true free space tolerated by caring individuals. For the child to play, the caring and compassionate holding environment will remove all anxieties just as a caring mother or caregiver removes all impingements like loud noise, hunger, or any deprivation for baby to play (Winnicott, 1989).

At some point, the child allows the mother to play with her—that is, the child interacts with the mother. This paves the way for the child and mother to play together in a relational manner, allowing the child to develop a capacity for group relatedness. Play can unify and integrate the human personality. It is through play that a child is able to create the whole of her personality. Players know that sometimes they play alone, especially if they need to practice by themselves, and at other times they play with others. Sometimes they can have fun by playing with their inner critics, which is, having a fun conversation with themselves. Winnicott believes play has five stages.

The first stage involves play that occurs best in a situation where there is good- enough parenting or a good-enough holding environment (Winnicott 1982, 2005) that welcomes the child into the world, an environment in which there is trust (Winnicott 1956, 303). Trust allows the child to play.

Second, playing comes from the inner space, which is also one's inner self. It could be a "space of freedom" in which the child learns how to live imaginatively and purposefully. The inner space can be large and spacious so the child can invite others in or narrow and closed to others. It can feel love or hate. It can also feel secured or threatened. The inner space can feel isolated and depressed, numb, or compassionate. An inner space that is secure is able to trust and take risks and be vulnerable (Winnicott 1982).

Third, play is exciting because it involves the body (Winnicott 1989). It is exciting because the person, the person's body, and the potential space all become alive in the course of the playing.

The fourth stage of play is that the child plays alone in the presence of someone else (Winnicott 1990). The child also learns how to hold emotions. In a situation where the child cannot cope with anxiety, she runs to the mother to calm the anxiety and returns to play. For Winnicott, it is always important for a responsible person to be available when children play. He feels that the adult or other responsible person need not interfere in the child's effort by inserting themselves in the play activity.

In the fifth stage, the child needs to learn to play with others according to the rules of play. To play with others implies that the child must view her mother or caregiver as someone who is also able to play like the child (Winnicott 1968). When children gradually begin playing together, they are no longer strangers but friends, which also forms a community. Playing together becomes a life-giving activity and facilitates the forming of relationships. Playing aide us in moderating our emotions of anxiety as well as aggression.

## 5. The Capacity for Concern

This capacity describes the ability to manage one's anger or feelings of destructiveness toward others. Capacity for concern is the courage and ability to be responsible for one's own actions and then seek reparation. This is concern for the other person in word and deed, and when destructiveness occurs, it is to engage in reparation. When children are growing up, they may bite or hit another without any provocation. This is the start of the destructiveness that the child may grow out of or not. In the early life of a healthy infant, a very important stage of development is marked by the beginning of a capacity for concern. Children gradually develop a sense of personal responsibility for their actions. They develop a capacity to experience guilt in an infantile way. The baby gradually becomes aware of a "Me" as separate from "Not Me" and of the mother as a person with her own needs. The baby also becomes aware of feeling both hate and love toward the mother. As this awareness becomes refined, it leads to the appearance of concern. It is the mother's love and care over a course of time that allows the healthy infant to discover a personal desire to give, to construct, and to mend. This achievement of the capacity for concern requires the mother's capacity, first of all, to accept and tolerate the baby's natural loving and aggressive impulses, and second, to provide the general loving care and everyday management of the baby. As the baby grows, this innate sense of morality (Winnicott 1990) becomes refined as well. Winnicott believes that there needs to be an integration between the love and hate in the person because, if this is not done, those concerned put others who live in the same environment at risk of becoming victims of unacceptable behaviors and attitudes. The capacity for concern is seen in everyday life and, depending on what one chooses to or not do, will make a difference. Winnicott believes that when one hurts another and guilt feelings set in, that guilt feeling can be removed when person who caused the hurting repairs the damage-that is, the capacity for concern. Again, capacity for concern is present when an individual realizes that she is hurting another person and chooses to repair the damaged relationship. Therefore choosing to engage in an act of reparation is a sign of a mature person. It means that this individual has been able to gradually acknowledge her own cruelty. To desire to continue in one's capacity for concern is to continue to repair relationships and bring restitution to others. Sometimes we can find in others who deny personal destructiveness but can be very aggressive and react irrationally to a situation, showing anger that erupts like a volcano and then choosing to discipline others by shaming them. Expressing emotions in a healthy way is often foreign since doing so is not always encouraged or taught in many homes-certainly not in the convent. One needs to arrive with it (Winnicott).

## 6. The Capacity to Use Others and Be Used

The capacity to use others and also be used is the ability to risk your own vulnerability and allow others to be who they are. It would be unfortunate for one who lacks authenticity, vulnerability, and intimacy to relate to people guided by emotional and relational forces. Most often, people tend to see in others aspects of themselves they hate. An old African adage, when translated into English, reads, "The pot calls the kettle black," which brings out the meaning of this clearly. Both the pot and the kettle are black owing to continuous use over a coal or wood fire, and yet the pot has not noticed that it is black. It has only noticed the blackness of the kettle. Learning how to use another person in a relational setting allows for authenticity, in which the two are enriched by their experiences. An individual, especially one who chooses the religious life, who lacks the capacity of object usage will have an adverse impact on the apostolic life or ministry to the people. It is interesting to imagine the outcome or impact on the lives of the sisters if one religious sister chose not to consider other persons in the community as individuals made in the image and likeness of God as herself.

Winnicott sees his capacity to use others and be used in the same way in terms of the deep relationship between a mother and a baby-the holding environment that allows the baby to "use" the mother. There is mutual use of each other. The mother derives satisfaction from caring for the baby, and the baby feels satisfied by the mother's care. This is a situation in which a person is able to enter into a deep relationship with another person. It is not an exploitative use of another person (Winnicott 1982). Winnicott was also thinking of therapist-patient relationships, how a therapist would be able to hear the pain of the patient in such a way that the patient would be able to use the presence, therapeutic alliance, and words of the therapist to work through his or her issues for transformation.

A patient recounted why she had stopped attending church early in her life. The patient's mother had some nuns as her friends. The patient's baby sister died unexpectedly without being baptized, and so in her religion class, she asked the nun who was her teacher if her little sister would go to heaven or hell without baptism. She argued that her baby sister had not committed any sin.

The nun had to quote the Catechism of the Church and gave the patient all the theological reasons behind infant baptism and baptism in general. The patient reported that she was so confused and felt unsettled, and for many years she felt the nun had not heard her inner pain over losing her baby sister. The nun saw the question through a theological lens, and the patient could not put the nun "to use." There was a lack of the capacity to imagine. The nun could not imagine that the patient was grieving the loss of her baby sister and therefore went on with her theological presentation to a child of about seven years. The nun did not realize that questions often have a deeper motivation. Winnicott talks of two ways of engaging; one is object relating, the way one sees a person (1968). For example, the way a daughter sees and views her father when she is a child is different from how she views him as an adult. As a child, the daughter sees the father as the best father. The other way of engaging is object usage. In maturity, the child sees the father's real self, the real father with all his inabilities. It is important to note that the capacity to use others and to be used requires experiencing another person's ruthless behavior. This is sometimes in the form of words spoken to us by or that we speak to those to whom we minister. This idea of the capacity to useobjects is connected also to the capacity to play.

Hamman echoes Winnicott's truth by saying, "If these capacities are poorly developed, one can recognize that in the traits, behavior, and choices of a person" (2014, 210).

**Growth and Developmental Process of the Individual**

Everyone born must go through developmental stages to attain the personality that will be his or hers. This is true of individuals who will choose to become nuns or religious sisters. Each phase has its difficulties. If a phase is left unresolved, the other phases may be burdened with difficulties. If a phase is successfully navigated (Winnicott in his 1962 lecture, calls this integration) by the growing infant, the result is a healthy personality. Our focus is on the emotional development and growth of the individual; as an individual grows physically, we hope that she also grows psychologically. This growth and developmental process is seen as a journey the individual embarks upon, just as the religious life is a journey to be embarked upon by the individual sister. The individual's journey to the religious community starts at home, and the first home is the womb.

**The Place We Call Home**

Home is a crucial point of reference in memory. It is where our hearts are. Across cultures, people have homes. Home is a place where one lives, especially with members of a family or household. It is a place where we can just be ourselves. Home is a gathering place for family members, a shelter, and a safe sanctuary. It provides escape from daily life. Home is where one feels comfortable. It is a place one rests after a long day's work or a tiring journey and where one can be at peace. It is a place that provides hospitality, security, and care for the individual. Home is the loving, supportive environment in which one grows up. It is where one seeks empowerment and affirmation and where one feels connected to others. A home is where happiness and peace can happen. It is a place one feels content.

The home becomes unlivable if it becomes unstable. Any type of instability in the home of a child can have a great impact on the child's well-being. Children who go through the worst levels of neglect and abuse in the home often struggle to recover and live normal lives. This unstable home may also be the infant or child's home. It is important for the "emotional needs of a child to be met at home by loving parents" (Chapman and Campbell 2005, 144). We will look at this infant or child who finds herself in this unstable home atmosphere and her first home environment—which is the womb.

## The Womb: The First Home of the Individual

Children are primarily emotional beings, and their first understanding of the world is emotional. Recent studies have shown that the mother's emotional state affects the baby even in the womb. The fetus responds to the mother's anger or happiness. When the child is born and as she grows she is extremely sensitive to the emotional state of the parents.

The womb is where the fetus gets what it needs to grow. The womb is involved in providing nutrients and support to the developing embryo. It is the womb where the offspring is conceived and grown until birth. It is responsible for the development of the embryo and fetus. The womb, as a home, attempts to create a safe environment for the fetus to thrive into maturity. A different scenario develops if the mother did not want the pregnancy. Then the womb becomes an agent that is destructive to the fetus's very existence. The fetus may feel unsure of its safety, especially if the pregnancy has been tampered with (attempted abortion). Then the fetus's home becomes abusive and unpredictable. Will the growing fetus feel anxious at his or her birth if there have been any disruptions? How long can the child be affected if the mother did not want the pregnancy, attempted to abort the fetus, and was not successful? What will be the outcome of the relationship between the growing fetus and the mother, even after birth? Cameron believes that "the intrauterine development depends in the first place upon the goodness of its physiological interaction between mother and unborn child" (1963, 27). According to Ciara L. Anderson, "A mother's womb was designed by God as the first home of an unborn child (fetus). The womb is the primary source of shelter, sustenance, stability and safety for the child. While inside the mother's womb the child experiences early stages of life, growth, and comfort even if it causes discomfort to the mother" (Anderson 2008, 7). As the fetus grows, developing all of its internal organs, it also develops all kinds of external behaviors that the mother can feel. Arms and legs move about, hands can grasp, and so forth (Anderson 2008, 7). If the womb becomes destructive to the child and the fetus feels unsure of its safety, what happens to the emotional state of the growing fetus after it is born? Anderson, in *Drowning in Mother's Womb*, said this of herself: "No matter what I did to my outer appearance, on the inside I felt doomed like drowning in my mother's womb.... It makes me wonder if the doctor who delivered me into the world forgot to cut the umbilical cord. Now it has seemingly become a noose around my neck-strangling the life out of me" (Anderson 2008, 23).

To buttress this point, Colarusso in *Child and Adult Development* expanded on Freud's description of the period in the womb as "a time when the fetus, if only unconsciously, felt that he or she had everything desirable and that the time of birth was on magical... omnipotence, when the new infant tried to recapture the perfection of the womb" (1992, 30). This means that the environment in which the fetus carries out its vast developmental changes needs to be peaceful and not disruptive. Cameron describes the environment of the unborn child as thus: The child is protected from cold and heat, from bright lights and loud sounds, from blows and sudden stress. He dwells in a warm, dark chamber immersed almost weightlessly in a fluid, cushioned by it and provided through the placenta with continuous room service.... As long as the unborn child gets from his mother's blood what he requires for growth, maintenance and a little moving about, and as long as his waste products are removed fast enough, by the same route, he can have little experience with the tensions of physiological want that flood him after he is born. (1963, 28)

If a mother felt great distress about having to keep an unwanted pregnancy, how would she treat the growing fetus? Was a father present during the pregnancy? We will presume that the fetus feels safe. We may only speculate, especially if the mother did not want the pregnancy and felt unhappy about it. Bowlby argues that an "unwanted child is likely not only to feel unwanted by his parents but to believe that he is essentially unwantable, namely unwanted by everyone" (1973, 204). Brazelton and Crammer believe that "the earliest attachment may be said to begin here, for there is a separate being and the possibility of a relationship" (1990, 21). It is important to imagine whether sometimes religious sisters or nuns feel confident to call the convent their home or sometimes feel unwanted in the convent environment.

**Father's Presence or Influence**

These days most fathers are involved in planning for a baby. They participate in the prenatal visits and are often present at the birth. While a woman cannot flee from the fact of pregnancy, a father-to-be can choose the extent to which he wants to get involved. He could withdraw and ignore what is going on depending on how he feels regarding the pregnancy. He might feel that he was fooled, tricked, lured, or coerced into this pregnancy. And if he is involved, he may also feel excluded or displaced. "He may experience the child to come as a rival who robs him of his wife, the way his father or a sibling had robbed him of his mother in his own childhood" (Brazelton and Cramer 1990, 37). Brazelton and Cramer, quoting Barnard (1982), state that the father's involvement in pregnancy and delivery reinforces his own identity as a participative active agent, lessening the likelihood of his exclusion (1990, 37). The father-to-be's emotional support during the woman's pregnancy contributes to her successful adaptation to the pregnancy. Brazelton and Cramer add that "recognition of a father's role helps a mother see the baby as separate from herself. If she remains aware that her pregnancy resulted from an act on the father's part as well as her own... of the father's wish for a child, she will avoid falling a prey to the illusion that she alone produced the baby" (1990, 22).

If the child finds out that the father and mother had no relationship and the father felt surprised to hear that the sexual relationship had resulted in pregnancy, it can be traumatic for the child, who will now believe that neither parent wanted her. "If the relationship with the father has been fraught with mainly resentment and conflict, this may be projected unto the child to be but if the relationship with the mother is sound, if the father endorses his responsibility as a co-creator and does not flee from his role, the mother will have a better chance of recognizing that the child is a separate being with a separate potential for growth" (Brazelton and Cramer 1990, 23). They add that if the father stays involved in a close love relationship with his wife, this will help to prepare her to renounce the gratification of an exclusive attachment to her baby (44). A child may feel abandoned if the father has no role in her life. The child may never feel close to her father.

Chapman and Campbell agree that "increasing attention is focused on the fathers' role in the development of their children" (2005, 143). They add that their "eleven-year study showed that greater attention from fathers resulted in less delinquent behavior and higher levels of education for the children. While the children get blamed for delinquent behavior, it is usually the fathers who are the delinquent ones in relation to the children" (143). They emphasized that "the stronger the emotional bond between children and their fathers, the less likely the children were to engage in delinquent behavior" (143). For them, if a child is "distressed with anxiety or melancholy, or feels unloved, she ... will have problems with concentration and attention span and feel a decrease in energy. It will be more difficult for her to keep her mind on the task at hand.... She will be ... preoccupied with her emotional needs" (143).

The British object relations theory is a "system of inbuilt parts of personality in relation to each other inside the self.These are expressed in the arena of current relationships by which the original intrapsychic construction of object relations is further modified" (Scharff and Scharff 1997, 4). This means that we model our current relationships on what we have internalized or taken into the infant psychic structure. So, when there is fighting and chaos in the home, when adults push their frustration and anger on the growing child and belittle the child with phrases like "Be grateful that I am caring for you" or "Be grateful that I have cared for you since your father left," the child will internalize all these statements. The child will internalize a mother's or caregiver's neglectful attitude, abuse, and drunkenness if they are a part of her household dynamics.

Fairbairn, who coined the term object relations, states that "libido is not primarily pleasure seeking but object-seeking" (1994, 137). Fairbairn believes that the purpose or goal of the libido is the object, and if the object is emotionally responsive, it means the child will have a love response. The infant is completely dependent on her object, which is the caregiving person, not only for her existence and physical well-being but also for the satisfaction of her psychological needs. The infant has no choice but to reject or accept the alternative of life and death (47). Fairbairn used a clinical case to illustrate his point on object relations as object seeking. The patient, as Fairbairn theorized, remarked, "You're always talking about my wanting this and that desire satisfied but what I really want is a father" (1992, 137). For Fairbairn, "the greatest need of a child is to obtain conclusive assurance that he is genuinely loved as a person and that his parents genuinely love him" (1992, 39).

When this assurance falls short, "his relationship to his objects is fraught with too much anxiety over separation" (1992, 39). Fairbairn viewed development as a gradual process during which individuals evolve from a state of complete, infantile dependence on the caregiver toward a state of interdependence, in which they still depend on others but are also capable of being relied upon. He confirms that a relationship with a bad object is felt by the child to be not only intolerable, but shameful Greenberg and Mitchell affirm that "when there has been unavailable or arbitrary parenting... there is profound disturbance in relating" (1983, 156).

According to Winnicott, "a baby can be fed without love, but loveless or impersonal management cannot succeed in producing a new autonomous human child" (1982, 146).

Winnicott discusses aspects of satisfactory parental care and groups them into three categories: first is "holding," second is "mother and infant living together," and third is "though the infant will not know that father is around, it ought to be father, mother and infant living together" (1965, 43). "Recently studies have shown that a father has direct influence on the child's development, but a mother can interfere with this bond between infants and their fathers. Mothers are gate keepers, capable of enhancing or dampening father-infant attachment. If they promote a triangle, this opens the way for the child's future attachment." Winnicott believes that good health is not possible if things do not start well enough for a child. "There is no possibility whatever for an infant to proceed from the pleasure principle to the reality principle or towards and beyond primary identification..., unless there is a good- enough mother. The good-enough mother is one who makes active adaptation to the infant" (2005, 13). He adds that "the mother adapts to the needs of her baby and of her child who is gradually evolving in personality and character and this adaptation gives her a measure of this reliability. The baby's experience of this reliability over a period of time gives rise in the baby and ... the growing child to a feeling of confidence. The baby's confidence in the mother's reliability, and therefore in that of the other people and things, makes possible a separating-out of the not me from the me" (Winnicott 1982, 147).

## The Birth and Attachment of the Individual

Cameron states,

Birth expels the child from the warm dark monotony of the uterine waters unto a world of everlasting change and infinite space. He is exposed to... taste and smell, to warmth and cold. He breathes the air, lies on solid surfaces, is picked up bodily and put down, carried around and handled in unfamiliar ways. The child experiences hunger and learns to ease himself through his own actions. To get food he must learn the art of sucking and swallowing while he breathes. He must digest and assimilate the food he takes in and eliminate waste product by his own muscular efforts. All this means work, and often it means discomfort, emptiness and pain. (1963, 28-29).

For Brazelton and Cramer, it is important to remember that infants bring their own characteristics to the relationship. It is a combination of the infant's makeup and specific style of behavior and the mother's interpretation of them that shapes their interaction (1990, 152). The infant during this time is very dependent on the caregivers. "They are helpless and cannot fend for themselves, the baby is incapable of any genuine interpersonal relationship. Apart from his feeding periods he remains for the most part a passive and isolated object of maternal care and affection, he must acquire a capacity for mutual interaction. As he develops perceptual, emotional, cognitive and motor abilities, he grows more and more capable of participating actively in the relationship which his mother offers" (Cameron 1963, 55). "As the infant matures it needs to form an intimate attachment to a mother figure. They are not born with such attachment. They must develop it with their other's help, as they organize their earliest experience into primitive perceptual world" (40).

Attachment theory concerns emotional relations among humans. It postulates that children's interactions with their primary caregivers during infancy shape their help-seeking and attachment behaviors as well as their internal representations of themselves and of caregivers. John Bowlby, a British psychologist, psychiatrist, and psychoanalyst, developed the theory of attachment. He investigated infants' attachments to their mothers as well as the negative consequences of being separated from their mothers. His theory emphasizes different stages of separation anxiety. He proposed that early attachment experiences result in children's organizing their views of themselves as either lovable or unlovable and their attachment figures as either trustworthy or untrustworthy. He believes that the attachments formed during childhood have an impact in adulthood.

Attachment theory states that "a young child needs to develop a relationship with at least one primary care giver for social and emotional development to occur normally. Without that care, the child will often face permanent psychological and social impairment" (Bowlby 1982, 3-7). He adds, "Although there are many differences of detail between species, maintenance of proximity by an immature animal to a preferred adult, almost always mother, is the rule, which suggests that such behavior is survival value" (Bowlby 1979, 156). He observed that children, and humans in general, go through reactions when separated from their primary caregivers. From such observations, Bowlby realized that, for bonding to take place, "an infant must be more than a mere passive receptor to the caregiver's behavior"

(Feist and Feist 2009, 153). The two must be responsive to each other. This realization resulted in birth to attachment styles, which Mary Ainsworth and her researcher developed.

One of the assumptions of attachment theory is that a "bonding relationship' (or lack of it) becomes internalized and serves as a 'mental working model' on which future relationships and love relationships are built. The bonding attachment is, therefore, the most critical of all relationships" (Feist and Feist 2009, 153). Bowlby states, "If attachment goes well, there is joy and a sense of security, if it is threatened, there is anxiety and anger. If it is broken, there is grief and depression" (Bowlby 1988, 4). A growing child remembers her mother regardless of who she is. The child will be grateful for just one person and cannot afford to be angry. She can sacrifice her anger, for example, over being abandoned and turn it on herself. No wonder this individual can experience chronic depression and anxiety. The mother's unavailability may make the individual attach to whomever is present, even if they are dysfunctional.

Hungarian clinical professor and analyst Margaret Schoenberg Mahler declared that, for a child to reach psychological birth and individuation, the child need to go through three developmental stages (1972). These stages take place in phases, each with several sub phases. These stages are as follows:

Normal autistic phase: First few weeks of life

Normal symbiotic phase: Lasts until about five months of age

Separation-individuation phase: Marks the end of the normal symbiotic phase

According to Mahler, successful completion of the developmental stages in the first years of life results in separation individuation. *Separation* refers to the development of limits, such as the separation between the infant and the mother. It refers to an internal process of mental separation from the mother, while *individuation* refers to a developing self-concept. It is the development of the infant's ego, with a sense of identity as well as cognitive abilities. Even though it is interrelated, it is possible for one to develop more than the other, largely depending on the mother's attitude toward the child. Mahler speculates in her theory, "After the first few weeks of infancy, in which the infant is either sleeping or barely conscious-normal autism (3 or 4 weeks)... the 'newborn' infant satisfied. various needs within the all-protective orbit of a mother's care (1972, 741). This is because an infant cannot tend to its own needs and has to rely on her caregiver. The infant from this time progresses from the normal symbiotic phase (five months), in which she perceives herself as one with her mother within the larger environment. During this period, the "infant behaves and functions as if... she and mother are a dual unity within one common boundary" (741). The mother can sense the child's feelings of distress, pain, or hunger, and the child is able to send these cues to the mother. The last stage is separation individuation (thirty to thirty- six months). This is the period in which children separate psychologically from their mothers, achieve a sense of individuation, and develop a personal identity. Mahler states that separation and individuation are conceived as two complementary developments: separation consist of the child's emergence from symbiotic fusion with the mother... and individuation consists of those achievements marking the child's assumption of her own individual characteristics (1975, 4).

Mahler divides the separation-individuation phase into three sub phases (1972).

1. Hatching (five to nine months): The infant gradually becomes aware of the differences between herself and the mother. The

infant becomes more aware of her surroundings and is interested in them, and so she uses the mother as a point of reference.

2. Practicing (nine to fourteen months): In this period, the infant can get around on her own by crawling and then walking.

It is a time for the infant to explore and become independent of the mother, even though she experiences herself as one with her mother.

3. Rapprochement (fifteen months and beyond): Even though the young child feels close to her mother, she begins to differentiate herself from her mother and at the same time wants to keep her mother in sight so that, through eye contact and action, she can explore the world. The child reaches back to the mother if she encounters challenges in the environment.

Mahler further divides rapprochement into three sub stages.

1. Beginning: The young child has this motivation to share her discoveries with mother.

2. Crisis: The child is conflicted or torn between staying connected to another and venturing out and becoming more independent in her adventures and discoveries.

3. Solution: This is a time when the child resolves the crisis or the conflict, according to her own newly formed individual, using her new, gradually fledgling language and her interactions with the temperament of her mother (1972, pp. 333-338). She believes that disruptions in the fundamental process of separation-individuation could result in a disturbance later in life in the ability to maintain a reliable sense of individual identity.

Therefore, if a growing child had felt unwanted and had struggled to be wanted and loved, where will she spend her energy except in the continuation of the struggle to be loved by a mother or father? What will be the implication for a growing child who believes that she is a fault? If a mother consistently tells a growing child, "You ruined my life," just because the mother was unprepared for the pregnancy, how fair is this to the child? If a mother scapegoats a growing child for her pregnancy, what a burden it is for this growing child. Fairbairn suggests, "Such experience of humiliation and shame reduce the child to a state of worthlessness....The child feels bad, inferior" (1952, 113). John Bradshaw, in his book *Healing the Shame That Binds You*, states, "I am flawed and defective as a human being. I am a mistake" (2005, 31). This will be how this child will see herself going forward.

**Different Attachment Styles of the Growing Child**

The need for attachment according to Bowlby "is to be protected from predators" (1988, 3). He is particularly concerned about the attachment between the infant and the mother. He says, "If it goes well, there is joy and a sense of security. If it is threatened, there is jealousy, anxiety and anger. If broken, there is grief and depression" (4). He continues to say, "No parent is going to provide a secure base for his growing child unless he has an intuitive understanding of and respect for his child's attachment behavior" (12). He adds that a child needs three basic things:

1. The child has need for food and warmth. When a mother meets these basic needs and the baby finds the source gratifying, the baby gets attached to the mother.

2. Infants have a built-in desire to relate and attach to their mothers' breasts to suck it and process it orally. In due course the infant attaches to the breast and the mother.

3. An infant has a built-in desire to be in touch with and to cling to a human being independent of food (Bowlby 1982, 178).

There are also three different attachment styles that infants adopt (Bowlby 1988; Ainsworth 1978): secure, anxious-resistant, and anxious-avoidant. Anxious-resistant ambivalent infants seem to be hypervigilant about maintaining contact with their mothers. They cling more intensely to their mothers after separation. They are not easily comforted and exhibit inhibited play behavior when separated from their mothers. Mothers of these infants have corresponded inconsistently with their babies so that the babies seem to respond by reacting to even mildly stressful situations with constant demand for attention and care. In anxious- resistant ambivalent attachment style, infants are ambivalent. They get conflicting messages from their caregivers. They are not certain whether their parents will be available or sensitive to their needs. This uncertainty gives rise to anxiety. The child tends to be clingy and is anxious about exploring the world (Bowlby 1988). In the anxious-avoidant style, the infant "accepts, stay calm when her mother leaves; they accept the stranger, and when their mother returns, they ignore and avoid her" (Feist and Feist 2009, 154). Infants show little interest in the presence or absence of their mothers while at play.

They display little distress upon separation from their mothers and tend to ignore their mothers upon reuniting with them. Mothers of these children tended to neglect their attachment needs. The children have no confidence that the mothers will respond to their needs, so they try to become emotionally self- sufficient. Both styles are insecure attachments. Secure infants play actively in their mothers' presence. They show some distress and reduce play behavior when separated from their mothers but are easily comforted by their mothers once reunited with them. Mothers of these infants tended to be sensitive and responsive to the infants' communication signals, which Ainsworth terms a "secure base" from which the infants can freely explore the world. In secure attachment, children are confident that their parents will be responsive, available, and helpful, especially when confronted with any adverse or frightening situations.

The parents, especially the mothers in the early years, are readily available, sensitive to their children's signals, and lovingly responsive when they seeks protection and comfort (Bowlby 1988). Ainsworth et al. provide a description of infants and their mothers that underscores the interactional nature of attachment style and gives powerful examples of how behavior, emotions, and cognition lead to the development of internal working models (1978). Infants experience of their mothers while at play. They display little distress upon separation from their mothers and tend to ignore their mothers upon reuniting with them. Mothers of these children tended to neglect their attachment needs. The children have no confidence that the mothers will respond to their needs, so they try to become emotionally self- sufficient. Both styles are insecure attachments. Secure infants play actively in their mothers' presence. They show some distress and reduce play behavior when separated from their mothers but are easily comforted by their mothers once reunited with them. Mothers of these infants tended to be on infant attachments has led to important theories about the powerful internal mental representations that influence relationships in adult life.

For Winnicott, the provision of a facilitating environment is nonnegotiable if the infant was expected to stay on the path of healthy development (1960). Winnicott believes that there is no such thing as an infant and that, without the mother's care, the infant would die, further asserting that "at the earliest stages the infant and maternal care belong to each other and cannot be disentangled" (1960, 40). Winnicott adds that the inherited potential of the infant was something that could unfold later and that the presence of the good-enough mother in these early stages "provide(s) a setting for the infant's constitution to begin to make itself evident, for the developmental tendencies to start to unfold" (Winnicott 1956, 303). He is even emphatic in a later paper when he states that he will countenance the idea of an inherited potential "provided that it is accepted that the inherited potential of an infant cannot become an infant unless linked to maternal care" (Winnicott 1960, 43). Forward echoed Winnicott's idea of a good- enough mother in a very simple way:

A good enough mother is not expected to be perfect and self-sacrificing to the point of martyrdom. She has her own emotional baggage, her own scars, her own needs. She may have work that doesn't want to compromise, and there may be times when she's not available to her daughter. She may lose her temper and say or do things to her daughter that she regrets. But if her dominant behavior engenders in her daughter a belief in her own value and nourishes her self-respect, confidence, and safety, that mother is doing a good job.... She is demonstrating real love, in a tangible, reliable way to her child. (Forward 2014, 3)

Winnicott also adds that "the mother who is not good enough is not able to implement the infant's omnipotence, and so she repeatedly fails to meet the infant's gestures instead she substitutes her own gestures which is to be given sense by the compliance of the infant. This compliance on the part of the infant is the earliest stage of the False Self and belongs to the mother's inability to sense her infant's needs" (2007, 147).

According to Erikson, when the attachment between mother and child is secure-that is, when the baby's needs are met-"his pleasure in being held, warmed, smiled at, talked to, rocked, and so forth, 'basic trust' is developed and is formed"

(1980, 61). Winnicott, in his book Playing and Reality, affirms that the first mirror of the infant is the mother's eyes or her whole face. This helps with the child's emotional development. If the mother's face is unresponsive or unwelcoming, the child investigates the mirror and finds its own face. The purpose of the child's looking into the mother's face (mirror) is to be noticed and get approval from her mother. "When I look, I am seen and so I exist. I can now afford to look and see" (Winnicott 1971, 149-154). If what the infant sees when she looks into her mother's face is only her moods or defenses, then she can lose track of the continuity of her being and miss out on a badly needed experience of omnipotence. The repetition of this experience of loss can lead to the infant's lack of creative capacity. It will also stifle the ability of the infant to perceive and tolerate the quiet moments of unintegration during the holding phase.

Winnicott constantly emphasizes the role of the mother in the early stages, and he repeats over and over throughout his writing his belief that "the good-enough mother ... starts off with an almost complete adaptation to her infant's needs" (Winnicott 1971, 10). He repeats it because none of the later developments (especially the separating of mother and infant) can come about without this phase being adequately traversed. In the beginning, the mother's provision of almost total adaptation provides the infant with the opportunity to have the illusion that the breast is part of and magically controlled by the infant (Winnicott 1962). He posits that there is no interchange between the mother and the infant in this early process, that the "infant perceives the breast only in so far as the breast could be created just there and then," and that "psychologically the infant takes from a breast that is part of the infant, and the mother gives milk to an infant as part of herself" (Winnicott 1971, 12).

It is these brief experiences of omnipotence that lay the foundations so that the "baby can [begin to] meet the reality principle here and there, now and then, but not everywhere at once" (Winnicott 1962, 57). In other words, the highly attuned adaptation of the mother in these early stages provides the infant with enough continuity of being that the disparate parts can begin to integrate. Winnicott characterizes infants in these early stages as always on the brink of unthinkable anxiety, sometimes further away and sometimes closer to the precipice, but always near to anxiety, almost going to pieces, falling forever, and having no relationship to the body (1962). Ogden sees in the mother's adaptation to her infant's needs her "insulating the infant in his state of going on being from the relentless and unalterable otherness of time" (2004, 1,350). For him, the mother's adaptation must protect the infant from the impingements of reality and, through providing an illusion that the world functions almost solely on the exigencies of the infant's needs, helps the maturational processes in fostering a sense of integration in the infant. Winnicott set up two alternatives for how an infant could exist in this early crucial time: being (continuity of) or annihilation. If the mother fails to sufficiently identify with her infant during the time of primary maternal preoccupation or provide the necessary adaptation, then the infant develops core pathology (Winnicott's paper of 1960, in the maturational processes and facilitating environment, 1990, 37-53).

**The Growth Journey of the Individual**

Every human being is on a journey regardless of culture, and in every journey is a purpose. We are all journeying to our destinations, though the destination may be different for each individual person. To me, life is about journeying, and hope is very essential in the process of journeying. Hope is an emotion characterized by the sense that one will have a positive experience. It is a belief that one can influence the experience in a positive way. In this journey there are sometimes repeated obstacles and roadblocks. We can get lost, confused, and disillusioned and even wonder where we are really heading.

**Call to the Journey**

The concept of a journey is the quest for truth and internal change, and this requires perseverance, heroism, and hope. The journey I talk about is a psychological journey. Our psychological development and growth from baby to adult is likened to a journey. It calls for ego development out of the first state of attachment to the mother or primary caregiver. It also calls for growing out of a sense of dependence on them to gain a sense of independence (Winnicott 1960). It brings an autonomous functioning and the ability to relate to others. In the process, one becomes an individual, an authentic or true self. The goal of the psychological journey is "separation individuation" (Mahler 1963) and the development of an autonomous, coherent, self-respecting self. It is an encounter with the true self (Winnicott 1965). The false self is not overwhelming and taking over the true self. A psychological journey, when done well, will bring a good fit between the false and the true self to enhance integrity and vitality (Bollas 1989).

The writer's calling as a religious woman required a physical journey of moving from her home to the convent, but it also required a true inner journey. This journey of transformation has to be taken if one desires wholeness. Winnicott adds that, without his six capacities enumerated, an individual develops a false self as opposed to a true self, which will aid that person in living a fuller life, even if it is the religious life (1960).

**True Self and False Self: Living for Others**

One of the most important concepts to emerge from Winnicott's examination of the consequences of the failures I environmental provision was the notion of the true and the false self (1960). The true self is also known as the real, authentic, original, and vulnerable self, while the false self is known as the fake, idealized, superficial, and pseudo self. These are psychological concepts that Winnicott introduced int psychoanalysis (1960). He coined the terms *true self* and *false self.* The true self springs from the inner spontaneity of the infant. The false self, on the other hand, springs from accommodating and responding to environmental demands. The problem with the false self is that one who puts that self forward tends to live life for others. Winnicott used the term in connection with the mother- infant dyad. The false self develops when the mother does not provide good-enough experiences for the infant (Winnicott 1960). Winnicott used true self to describe a sense of self based on spontaneous authentic experience and a feeling of being alive, of having a real self (Akhtar 2009, 128). The false self, by contrast, Winnicott saw as a defensive façade (Winnicott 1960, 140-157) that, in extreme cases, could leave its holders lacking spontaneity and feeling dead and empty behind a mere appearance of being real. The false self is a defensive mechanism with which the individual who prematurely took over the nursing and caring functions of the parent adapts. It hides the true spontaneous self. In some cases, the false self sets up a self that others may interpret as secure but may not be so at all. Let us think of a religious woman or sister who smiles when outside the convent premises but who has insecurities in the convent and so cannot produce that kind of smile. Winnicott saw the true self as rooted from early infancy in the experience of being alive, including blood pumping and lungs breathing-what Winnicott called simply being (Jacobus 2005, 160). Out of this, the baby creates a sense of reality, a sense that life is worth living. The baby's spontaneous, nonverbal gestures derive from that instinctual sense (Winnicott 1965, 121), and if parents respond to these gestures, they become the basis for the continuing development of the true self. The infant journeys from being very dependent on the mother to independence; therefore, satisfactory maternal care maintains the normal infant self. Winnicott, in *The Maturation Process and the Facilitating Environment,* states that "the true self does not become a living reality except as a result of the mother's repeated success in meeting the infant's spontaneous gestures or sensory hallucination" (1990, 145).

As the mother meets the needs of the infant, the infant's true self continues to grow. Similarly, the mother who is not able to meet the infant's needs is not good enough. When the good-enough mother can meet her infant's needs, the child begins to "enjoy his illusion of being omnipotent and magical" and this gives health. The good- enough mother is to attend to her infant in the day-to-day caregiving. The infant is to be the mother's preoccupation. Winnicott was careful to describe not a perfect mother but a good-enough one. If she is not able to meet her infant's needs, the infant grows and lives falsely. If good-enough parenting does not take place, the infant's spontaneity is in danger of being encroached on by the need for compliance with the parents' wishes and expectations. The environmental failure of the various stages of the child's development has a very serious effect on later development. The not-good-enough mothering could result in the creation of what Winnicott called the false self, where "other people's expectations can become of overriding importance, overlaying or contradicting the original sense of self, the one connected to the very roots of one's being" (Winnicott 1994, 241; quotes J. Klein). The infant can become compliant to the mother's needs. "The infant gets seduced into a compliance, and a compliant False Self reacts to environmental demands and the infant accepts the compliance. Through the False Self the infant builds up a false set of relationships, and by means of introjection even attains a show of the being real, so that the child may grow to be just like mother" (Winnicott 1990, 146). The danger Winnicott saw was that "through this false self, the infant builds up a false set of relationships, and by means of introjections even attains a show of being real (Winnicott 1990, 146) while, in fact, merely concealing a barren emptiness behind an independent- seeming façade (Minsky 2006, 119-120).

The main goal of the false self is to "hide the true self" (Winnicott 1960, 144). Even though the pathological false self stifles the spontaneous gestures of the true self in favor of a lifeless imitation, Winnicott nevertheless considered it of vital importance in preventing something worse: the annihilating experience of the exploitation of the hidden true self (Jacobus 2005). Winnicott, in his paper entitled "The Concept of a Healthy Individual," affirms the need for a traumatized child to hide behind the true self. He states, "I refer to those persons who have unconsciously needed to organize a false self-front to cope with the world, this false self being designed to protect the true self." Daniel Stern writes, "The parent must be able to read the infant's feeling state from the infant's overt behavior.... The parent must perform in some behavior that... corresponds in some way to the infant's overt behavior" (1973, 139). It is only through this process of attunement that the infant's spontaneity will be mirrored. Compliance gives way to false self and thus hide the true self. The growing child can develop defenses to protect herself. Winnicott adds that children's early experiences of their caregivers' responsiveness to feelings and needs compel them to shape themselves to be more acceptable to caregivers; in other words, when actual self-experiences are deemed unacceptable by others, children "split off" these aspects of their formative self-images as a protective strategy and to maintain their relationships (1960, 140-152).

Fromm distinguished the original self and the pseudo self, the inauthenticity of the latter being a way to escape the loneliness of freedom (1942). Carl Rogers, in his book On Becoming a Person, quoted Kierkegaard on this issue: "The most common despair is to be in despair at not choosing, or willing, to be oneself; but that the deepest form of despair is to choose 'to be another than himself.' On the other hand, 'To will to be that self which one truly is, is indeed the opposite of despair," (1961, 110). He added that "to remove a mask which you had thought was a part of your real self can be a deeply disturbing experience" (110). He postulated that "real person" consists of feelings that underlie a false front (Rogers 1961, 110). Miller warns that "a child/patient ... may not have any formed true self, waiting behind the false self-façade" (2004, 21) and as a result "freeing the true self is not as simple as the Winnicottian image of the butterfly emerging from its cocoon" (Malcom 1988, 135). Miller says again, "If a true self can be developed, however, she considered that the empty grandiosity of the false self could give way to a new sense of autonomous vitality" (Miller 2004, 45). The false self helps in life by assisting one in discerning what might be appropriate in a social context. For example, it stops one from popping gum in a job meeting if the individual likes to do this generally. Similarly, "It guides us towards a polite and mannered social attitude.... It defends the true self. The true self is inward turning whereas the false self, due to the compliant nature, is outward turning" (Hamman 2014, 59).

The concept of the true and false self- provided Winnicott with a means of characterizing many forms of psychopathology and with a tool with which to trace back the problem of those presenting for analysis to a point where the fault had occurred. Many religious women live in their various convents presenting their false selves because the true selves have diminished. Though much later, Erikson offered a concept equivalent to Winnicott's concept of the false self and true self.

Erikson, in 1966, presented the concept of pseudo-species as the result of the burden of "being alike."

What is at stake here is nothing less than the realization of the fact and the obligation of man's specieshood. Great religious leaders have attempted to break through the resistances against this awareness, but their churches have tended to rejoin rather than shun man's deepseated convictions that some providence has made his tribe and race or class, caste, or religion "naturally" superior to others. This seems to be part of a psychosocial evolution by which he has developed into pseudo-species... for man is not only apt to lose all sense of species, but also to turn on another subgroup with a ferocity generally, alien to the "social" world. (Erikson 1966, 442)

The point Erikson makes here is that the implication of pseudo-species (the dominance of the false self) can lead to the diminishing value of the personhood of the individual, and the false self does the same. The psychopathology that emerges from the true and false self-concept that Winnicott sought to address could be diagnosed in one's behavior. Behavior, simply put, is the way one acts or conducts oneself, especially toward others. The *APA Dictionary of Psychology* has two definitions for behavior: first, "an organism's activities in response to external or internal stimuli, including objectively observable activities, introspectively observable activities... and unconscious processes"; and second, "more restrictively, any action or function that can be objectively observed or measured in response to stimuli" (2007, 107). From these, we can safely say that we can observe actions or functions and say they are good behaviors proper or correct conduct) or not-so-good behaviors, or dysfunctional behaviors.

**Some Causes or Stages of Dysfunctional Behaviors**

Dysfunctional behavior, as I understand it, is impaired functioning on the part of an individual person in any sort of relationship. The poor functioning manifests in behaviors as well as relationships that are not working due to negative impacts. Behavioral issues like family conflicts or struggles with anxiety or poverty are some of the issues that could change behavior. A family is dysfunctional if it regularly experiences conflict, misbehavior, or abuse in a way that can cause disruptions in the family affairs. In convents or religious houses, such dysfunctions are sometimes displayed in such a manner that they cause disruptions in both prayer and apostolic life. Children raised in dysfunctional environments may believe that they are the cause of the situation, so they choose to be more compliant, more funny, or more pleasing to please the adults. These same behaviors are manifested in many convents where young nuns or those in formation try to be compliant to the point of losing themselves. A dysfunctional environment will always have a long-term effect on those living in it, even in adult life and even if the individual chooses to live in a healthier environment-or even when this individual chooses to enter the religious life as a religious sister or nun. Dysfunctional parents may have learned their behavior from their own parents and then reproduce these experiences in their new families. In the same vein, an individual who has learned these behaviors from her home atmosphere, even when she becomes a religious sister or nun, will reproduce these behaviors in the convent environment and cause everyone heartaches. Unfortunately, some children who grow up in such dysfunctional family situations believe that the situations or behaviors are normal and acceptable. Often in convents, sisters say, "This is who I am," thinking their behaviors are okay. Meanwhile, other sisters suffer from their ruthlessness. In dysfunctional families, there is lack of empathy, poor communication skills, most often emotional and physical abuse, and drug and alcohol use in abundance. In such homes, there are no boundaries, with control issues and negative criticisms being the order of the day. Similarly, in dysfunctional homes, children do not learn to stand up for themselves as they fear abandonment. Children of such homes are often given double messages and become people pleasers. At times, these children want to belong to someone else's family and are quick to blame others. (Refer to Katherine T. Owens's blog at http://www.a-spiritual- journey-of-healing.com.) Oftentimes, when sisters show a lack of empathy, have control issues, or criticize at random, one wonders where all the "prayers of their lives" went. These behavioral issues are much bigger than just following the daily routine prayers of the religious life. It is important at this juncture to turn to what Erik Erikson and Donald Winnicott have to say with regard to the formation of these behaviors.

## Erik Erikson and Donald Winnicott

Erik Erikson and Donald Winnicott believe that the eight stages of psychosocial development and the six capacities are contributing factors that shape a person's behavior. The stages of psychosocial theory break down are as follows:

### *Basic Trust vs. Basic Mistrust: Hope*

In the first stage of Erikson's psychosocial theory, basic trust versus basic mistrust (from birth to one year of life), he makes it very clear: "If the baby is fed, changed and feels safe in its environment the infant will rely on the sameness and continuity of the providers, it will trust others and herself that the 'world is good' but the amount of trust that develops in the infant depends on the quality of the mutual relationship" (1993, 240-249). Erikson feels that when parents present consistent, adequate, and nurturing care for a growing child, the child develops basic trust and realizes that people are trustworthy and dependable. This belief will make the child develop a sense of confidence. If the infant realizes that her mother provides food at regular times and attends to her needs regularly and with consistency, the infant will begin to learn basic trust; if the opposite is true, the infant will learn basic mistrust. Erikson enumerates the needs for food, sleep, feeling wanted, and inner goodness as well as an experience of sameness and continuity. Children develop a sense of trust when caregivers provide reliability, care, and affection. A lack of this will lead the child to feel mistrust.

To buttress this point, Winnicott states, "A holding environment affects both the emotional and mental development of the child. The term holding environment is used not only as the physical holding of the infant, but also the total environmental provision prior to the concept of living with" (2005, 43). It is this caring and compassionate holding environment that is needed before play can happen. The holding environment removes all anxieties and insecurities. To form emotional stability, a child needs to internalize a constant and positive image of the mother. This situation makes it possible for the child to function as a separate individual. If the child can achieve emotional constancy, a sense of self will be achieved as the child matures. A growing child depends upon her mother for further psychological and developmental growth to occur, just as in utero, the infant as fetus was dependent on her mother for physical growth. If a growing child sees only her face and not her face in her mother's (Winnicott 2002, 114), she will not have the capacity to develop basic trust. Winnicott's capacity to believe has to do with our being able to depend on and to provide the basis for others to depend on us. The capacity to believe in people is nurtured and greatly affected through our experience —that is, the early experience of the infant. It begins with the mother's interactions with the infant. In Winnicott's Home Is Where We Start From, he states that "a good enough environment, and the mother's maternal preoccupation" (1986,

22) provide this capacity to believe. "It is only on a continuity of existing that the sense of self, of feeling real and of being, can eventually be established as a feature of the individual personality" (22). This basic trust or basic mistrust and the capacity to believe makes faith possible in adulthood (Hamman 2014, 53). An emotionally unavailable mother will portray "absent mother merge," and this "makes a child feel and conclude maybe it would be better if I were not born" (Cori 2010, 24).

### *Autonomy vs. Shame and Doubt: Will*

The second psychosocial stage of Erikson's theory is autonomy versus shame and doubt (early childhood, eighteen months to three to four years). Erikson states that, at this point in the child's independence, when her environment urges her to "stand on her own, it must protect (the child) against meaningless and arbitrary experiences of shame and of early doubt" (1963, 252). Early childhood is when an infant begins to express herself as well as feel independent.

This is also the period when shame and doubt abound. It is a period during which parents try to inhibit infants' independence. Parents may shame their children for making a mess with their food or instill doubt through harsh questioning; they may rebuke their children's inability to do something or to meet parents' standards. "The conflict between autonomy and shame and doubt becomes the major psychosocial crisis for early childhood" (Feist and Feist 2009, 253). "Children who develop too little autonomy will have difficulties, lacking the basic strength of later stages" (Feist and Feist 2009, 253). Most parents remember that, when their children were quite young, two years old or so, they became surprisingly willful, grasping spoons and toys and ready to stand on their own feet. The stance is playful but firm and self- satisfying. Children want to demonstrate what they can do. The stronger the will is, the more they undertake. Since growth happens so quickly and generates such satisfaction, parents can only wonder and hope for their children's success. But there are limits. When these are overstepped and things get out of control, there may be a reversion to insecurity and a lack of self-confidence that ends in shame and doubt in their capacities (Erikson 1997, 107).

According to Erikson, "It is in this phase of development that the matter of mutual regulation between adult and child now faces its severest test" (1993, 70). Erikson believes that, in this period, parents should provide a facilitating environment in which the child can learn and gain control, thus building self-esteem. But if the parent is too rigid, harsh, and demanding, the child can feel defeated and experience extreme shame and doubt. Conversely, if the child is given no limits or guidance, the child can fail to gain any shame or doubt. Children who can express themselves freely gain autonomy and pride. Bowlby interviewed mothers regarding their childcare practices and found that the majority of them, if not all, use threats as a means of withdrawing love. Bowlby affirms that such an act destroys the child: "It takes the child's security away. You're the whole of their security and must not take that away" (1978, 229).

Winnicott suggests that trauma for a child means breaking the continuity of the child's existence (1990). Guntrip says that bad occurrences in infancy and childhood prevent children from developing a strong and consolidated ego structure, a firm sense of definite selfhood with positive characteristics and creative powers (Winnicott 1956, 137). Selma affirms this notion: "If we restrict a large part of his activity either, through our own exaggerated anxiety because his activity is a great trouble to us, we will run into another group of problems. If we follow him around in great fear... he will feel our anxiety and his own self confidence will suffer consequently" (Winnicott 1959, 90).

Winnicott's capacity to imagine speaks to the way one engages the outside world. It is being able to see what is not there, to hear what is not said, and to know what is unknown. The good-enough mother providing the holding environment can see and hear what the infant has not seen or said and be there for the infant. He adds that the growing infant "as they are in health ... is able gradually to meet the world and all its complexities... in ever widening circles of social life the child is identified with society" (Winnicott 1963, 91). "To be creative a person must exist and have a feeling of existing.... Creativity is then the doing that arises out of being" (Winnicott1963, 39). "Without a secure sense of being— the capacity to believe-imagination is a frightful experience of the unfamiliar and best be avoided" (Hamman 2014, 72). "Our ability to imagine makes it possible for us to entertain what is real and what is not so real" (Hamman 2014, 76). Living creatively and imaginatively is the ability to perceive reality, even when that part of reality is not yet realized. We need to live imaginatively and creatively in our everyday lives. Winnicott feels that "being and feeling real belongs essentially to health" (Winnicott 1986, 35). But "a whole life may be built on the pattern of reacting to stimuli. Withdraw the stimuli and the individual has no life" (Winnicott 1986, 39). He also believes that the infant's experience of the capacity to imagine starts with the child's believing that she "created the breast" even though it already existed (Winnicott 1986). Winnicott says that the capacity to imagine is the "retention throughout life of something that belongs to infant experience: the ability to create the world....Creativity means seeing everything afresh all the time 'with new eyes'" (Winnicott 1986, 49). He adds that every living person can live creatively irrespective of age. A growing child being allowed to use her creative imagination is healthy. There is the beginning of fantasy play, role play, and make-believe. Without the capacity to imagine, one will not be curious to explore a personal life narrative since such exploration will lead to one's own insecurities and anxieties.

During this period, children also have an increased interest in playmates other than their mothers (Mahler 1975, 116-117). if caregivers encourage self-sufficient behavior, children develop a sense of autonomy, a sense of being able to handle many problems on their own. On the other hand, if caregivers demand too much of children too soon or refuse to let them perform tasks of which they are capable of and ridicule early attempts at self- sufficiency, children may develop doubt and shame about their ability to handle problems. Selma adds, "Parental wisdom and understanding in the conduct of feeding, toilet training... discipline, serves the child's mental health by promoting his love and confidence in parents and by strengthening his own equipment in regulating his body needs and impulses" (1959, 94). When we understand the importance of imagination for mental health, we can draw certain inferences for child rearing. Selma states, "What we do to promote the creative and intellectual problem-solving abilities of the child will also promote the child's mental health... if we also take care not to make excessive or unreasonable demands upon the child" (1959, 5).

### *Initiative vs. Guilt*: **Purpose**

The next phase of Erikson's psychosocial stage is initiative versus guilt. This is also the play age. Erikson believes that this period (age three to six years) is about autonomy and the free possession of surplus energy in the child (1963). He states, "Initiative adds to autonomy the quality of understanding, planning and 'attacking' a task for the sake of being active and on the move" (1963, 255). It is a period in which the child becomes curious about her environment. She moves freely, and language develops. Play becomes more purposeful and constructive. To initiate suggests moving out into a new direction. It may be a lonely trip and still be successful, or it may be a move that catches the interest and participation of others. An initiative instigator is also often left with a sense of inadequacy and guilt (Erikson, 1963).

Winnicott states that play gives the child the necessary practice to manipulate objects. The child specializes in the management of aggression and destructiveness (1994, 60). "Play is basically a creative activity; but inadequate capacity make capacity to play diminish.... This produces lack of trust" (1994, 60). Winnicott believes that there is an achievement in the emotional development of every human child (1994, 59). He feels play is universal and is part of health: "Playing facilitates growth and therefore belongs to health. Playing leads nto relationship, playing can be a form of communication. Most importantly it implies trust" (Winnicott 2002, 59). He also believes,

"Play is primarily a creative activity ... under conditions in which the child is confident in someone or has become confident generally through adequate experiences of good care" (Winnicott 1989). By contrast, inadequate care produces a lack of trust, making the capacity to play unattainable. Winnicott argues that, through play, the child deals with external reality creatively. In the end, this produces creative living, which "leads to the capacity to feel real and to feel life can be used and enriched, without play the child is unable to see the world creatively, and in consequence is thrown back on compliance and a sense of futility, or on the exploitation of instinctual satisfaction" (Winnicott 1989, 60). He further observed in his "capacity to play' that there is first pleasure and second satisfaction. One can play with others, one can play according to rules and one can play with rules and regulations pre-arranged" (1994, 59). Since violence can happen during play it is proper to integrate both love and hate as well as acts of reparation, which is in the capacity for concern. Play depends on the achievements of the other capacities.

Winnicott asserts that "playing is an experience, always a creative experience and it is... a basic form of living" (1982, 67). Playing turns out best in situations where there is a good-enough holding environment, where parenting is good enough. In this holding environment is trust and confidence between the infant and caregiver or mother. It is this environment that will produce the capacity to believe. Winnicott states, "Play is always exciting. It is exciting not because of the background of instincts but ... it always deals with the knife-edge between the subjective and that which is objectively perceived" (Winnicott 1989, 205). It is true that play is exciting, and as it includes the whole of the person, this means that the capacity for concern is needed since being alive includes ruthless feelings as well. Winnicott writes, "Playing becomes an expression in terms of external material of inner relationships and anxieties" (1989, 60). Playing can tell something of who we are depending on our inner space's condition and size. Winnicott believes that playing has some healing essence or value. The creative aspect of play informs one's healing. He states, "It is in playing, and only in playing, that the individual child or adult is able to be creative and to use the whole personality, and it is only in being creative that the individual discovers the self" (Winnicott 1982, 73).

Hamman adds that Winnicott's "capacity to play embodies all the other capacities" (2014, 174). He says, "The ability to move effortlessly between illusion and reality and to lose oneself spontaneous, or purposive in activity. This in-between play space...is welcoming, forgiving, and nurturing space....It is also a vulnerable space" (174). In playing, one "needs the capacity to believe since playing brings excitement and vulnerability to one's being.... Playing requires the capacity to imagine.... Play can escalate into violence; it benefits from integration of love and hate and the act of reparation within the capacity for concern.... You need to discern whether you will play alone or with others ... and if you can use others and be used" (176).

Erikson affirms that the "child of four and five having found a firm solution to his problem of autonomy is faced with the next step and with the next crisis. Being now convinced that he is a person, the child must now find out what kind of person he is going to be" (1980, 78). The child at this stage learns basic skills-for example, how to zip and tie and count. The child wants to complete her own actions for a purpose. Activities involved in this may include risk-taking behaviors, perhaps wanting to cross streets alone. Because of initiative, the child may develop negative behaviors because she is developing a sense of frustration over not being able to achieve a goal as planned. She may engage in negative behaviors that seem aggressive, ruthless, and overly assertive to parents or caregivers. If parents are understanding and supportive of a child's efforts to show initiative, the child develops purpose, sets goals, and acts in ways to reach them, but if the child is punished for showing initiative, the child develops guilt (Erikson, 1980).

One child described an experience of punishment when she, at six years old, tried to assist her four-year-old sibling. She stated that her mother would lock the door and beat her with a cane until it broke, and then she would switch to a belt. She remembers crying until she could cry no more. She always wondered about her mother's harsh treatment of her. To her mother, she was a mistake (experience of a child). Alice Miller states, "Study of cruelty to children reveals people only mistreat their children if they have been victims of cruelty themselves"

(1998, 6). Too much purpose and guilt feelings lead people to exhibit ruthlessness, achieving all goals without caring upon whom they trample. Erikson states that the child needs to be accepted, affirmed, and nurtured in such a way that provides the tools for growth to the next stage of development (1980). Judith Herman adds,

The child trapped in an abusive environment is faced with formidable tasks of adaptation. She must find a way to preserve a sense of trust in people who are untrustworthy, safety in a situation that is unsafe, control in a situation that is terrifyingly unpredictable, power in a situation of helplessness. Unable to care for or protect herself, she must compensate for the failures of adult care and protection with the only means at her disposal, an immature system of psychological defense. (1997, 96)

Erikson adds that the "consequences of the guilt aroused on this stage ... often do not show until much later, when conflict over initiative may find expression in a self- restriction and this keeps an individual from living up to his inner capacity or powers of his imagination and feeling" (1980, 85).

To buttress this point, Winnicott emphasized that, if "an external sense of morality is forced upon a child too soon to control or even break the child's willful ruthlessness it can come at a cost for the 'capacity for concern.'"" He stressed that the capacity for concern needs to be cultivated by the growing child as she begins to negotiate her environment. For him, the capacity for concern "can be described in terms of the mother infant relationship" (Winnicott 1990, 74). He goes on further to explain in the paper he presented in 1963 that concern "refers to the fact the individual cares or minds, and both feel and accepts responsibility" (73). He explains, for example, that after intercourse, both parties need to take responsibility in case the act results in pregnancy. "Capacity for concern is at the back of all constructive play and work. It belongs to the normal life of the individual" (73).

Hamman, quoting Winnicott, states, "The capacity for concern describes your ability to feel and own your ruthlessness and your lack of compassion and it anticipates reparation and restitution of lives and relationships. This ability is greatly determined by the holding environment that received you" (2014, 92). "Some aspects of the origins of concern," Winnicott observes, happen "in the early stages in which the mother's continued presence has a specific value for the infant" (Winnicott 1990, 77). "Owning your destructiveness as a fundamental part of who you are might be one of the most difficult achievements in life" (Hamman 2014, 95). Since we are seldom taught how to own our emotions, Hamman writes about Winnicott's description of the guilt feelings young people go through when they feel they have hurt someone they love (2014, 98). The guilt feelings are removed when the damage is repaired. Therefore, "concern is not possible without the realization that we cannot control others in our omnipotence and as such is an integral part of settling on a sense of self" (Hamman 2014, 99).

Winnicott states, "Failure of the environmental mother to provide reliable opportunity for reparation leads to a loss of the capacity for concern, and its replacement by crude anxieties and by crude defences such as splitting and disintegration" (1990, 78). He adds, "In the initial stages of development, if there is no reliable mother- figure to receive the reparation gesture, the guilt becomes intolerable, and concern cannot be felt." (82) And concern goes with reparation. Individuals without the capacity for concern induce shame without even recognizing the hurt they cause. Without the capacity for concern, one will halt one's intervention, which emotionally will feel like hating the other and not responding to her needs (Winnicott 1990).

### *Industry vs. Inferiority: Competence*

Erikson calls his next stage of development industry versus inferiority. This occurs during children's school years (ages six to twelve years). Throughout their school years, children continue to develop self-confidence and start doing things on their own. They are eager to learn. Erikson calls this stage "entrance into life," explaining, "The child must forgo past hopes and wishes while his exuberant imagination is tamed and harnessed.... He now learns to win recognition by producing things" (1963, 258– 259). Industry and competence are aptitudes we all know about in this competitive world. "What one is good at, what is good for are the first queries of a fellow human being. Our schools start off that way, and we seldom recover the playfulness that led to the original creativity. We are all graded on our competence....In truth everything one does or attempts to do demands a standard of competence.in order to be accepted" (Erikson 1997, 109). Understandably it is necessary to be competent in order to excel in our practical world.

Erikson posits that, at "this stage the child develops a sense of industry and starts to be productive" (1963, 258-259). He continues, "The child now wants to be shown how to get busy with something and how to be busy with others" (Erikson 1980, 87). Erikson adds that the "danger at this stage is the development of a sense of inadequacy and inferiority" (1980, 91) in the child. If the child is not certain of his skills and despairs of his tools and skills, he may be discouraged from identification with them (Erikson 1963). Consider this example of one child: Her mother did not stop the harsh treatment she meted out to her. With the birth of her sister, the neglect she received was worse. For this reason, this child could not love her sister because her mother preferred the sister this child. Her sister was the perfect child, and this child the mistake. Mother blamed her for every wrong, so she spent her whole life struggling for attention from her mother. It was so tiring and hurtful. (Patient, conversation with researcher, 2017)

Winnicott feels that the capacity to be alone is one of the most important signs of emotional maturity in the development of the child at this period (1990). For him, the capacity to be alone is linked with self- discovery and self-transformation (1990). He adds that the capacity to be alone is very important because "without the sufficiency of it," there is no maturity. "The capacity to be alone does not come about"; it needs to be cultivated. He states, "This experience is that of being alone, as an infant and small child, in the presence of mother" (1990, 30). "Being able to enjoy being alone along with another person who is also alone... is an experience of health" (1990, 31). He explains that "the ability to be truly alone has as its basis in the early experience of being alone in the presence of someone... when the ego. immaturity is naturally balanced by ego- support from the mother. In the course of time the individual introject the ego- supportive mother and in this way becomes able to be alone without frequent reference to the mother or mother symbol" (1990, 32). The capacity to be alone describes one's ability to contain emotions and appetites and to enter appropriate relationships with others (Hamman 2014, 114). It allows one to become emotionally present to another. This period allows children to share and cooperate with others, and therefore children need to be praised for their accomplishments; but if they are ridiculed and punished for their efforts, they develop inferiority and a lack of motivation. While the capacity to be alone is the ability to be alone with oneself in the presence of others, it is not about loneliness. but about how emotions and thoughts are handled or contained appropriately. This capacity allows one to be alone with one's inner critic, alone with one's emotions and desires, and alone with the ruthlessness one experiences from others (Hamman 2014), especially as it often happens in religious houses. Without this capacity, people can be a danger to others and to themselves. Those who lack the capacity to be alone cannot keep confidentiality and cannot keep solitude. They use prayer and scriptures as a defense mechanism and have need for more relationships. If one cannot use others and be used, if individuals remain things and do not become people created in the image and likeness of God, then play activity also becomes a problem.

### *Identity vs. Role Confusion: Fidelity*

The next phase Erikson stipulates is identity versus role confusion (twelve to eighteen years of age, or to twenty-five years). It is a crucial period in the psychosocial stage of development. When children reach teenage years, they start to care about how they look to others. They start forming their identities by experimenting with who they are. This stage has a certain unique quality in a person's life; it is a bridge between childhood and adulthood. The adolescent passes through from puberty to adulthood with all its confusions." This stage of development is where "childhood proper ends with the advent of puberty" and youth begins (Erikson 1963, 261). Identity marks, acclaims, and distinguishes each person at birth and is immediately confirmed by naming. A boy gets a boy's name and a girl gets a girl's name. In the long run, it is only having a genuine sense of who we are that keeps our feet on the ground and our heads up to an elevation from which we can see clearly where we are, what we are, and what we stand for (Erikson, 1982). Puberty is a time for the genital organ to reach maturity. Both males and females grow pubic hairs, and it is a time for sexual interest. Not only that, but "there is a physical transition from immature to mature body" (Colarusso 1992, 92). There is also a psychological change. The mind develops the ability to integrate the changes in relationship to oneself and to others. If the child has been able to establish good relationships with parents and succeeded in gaining some social skills and sharing with others, she is considered developmentally healthy.

Erikson characterizes adolescence as the period in the human life cycle during which the individual must establish "a sense of personal identity and avoid the dangers of role diffusion and identity confusion" (1963, 262). According to Muuss in Theories of Adolescence, Identity achievements imply that the individual assesses strengths and weaknesses and determines how he or she wants to deal with them. The adolescent must find an answer to the identity question: who am I? Identity or sense of sameness and continuity must be searched for. Identity is not readily given to the individual by the society, nor does it appear as maturational phenomena when the time comes, as do secondary sex characteristics. Identity must be acquired through sustained individual efforts. Unwillingness to work actively on one's identity formation carries with it the danger of role diffusion, may result in alienation and a sense of isolation and confusion. (1972, 52)

Again, Muuss, who wrote about adolescent development, affirms, "Many of the social and behavioral problems adolescents encounter (substance abuse, dropping out of school)... can be viewed as reflecting earlier difficulties with mistrust, shame and doubt, guilt and/ or inferiority feelings" (1972, 53). When a child is not seen (Winnicott 1982) or has no place, voice, or identity and cannot express how she feels in the family, especially in cases of remarriage by either parent, she is bullied, put down, and criticized, and her identity will be compromised. When children are dominated for so long, they easily become doormats, unable to stand up for themselves.

### *Intimacy vs. Isolation: Love and Young Adulthood*

The next developmental stage Erikson describes is intimacy versus isolation (twenty-five to forty years old). The years of intimacy and love are bright and full of warmth and sunlight. To love and find oneself loved by another is to gain fulfillment and delight (Erikson 1982). Intimacy is the ability to be close, loving, and vulnerable. It is based in part upon identity development, in that one has to know oneself to share it. Failure to develop intimacy can lead to getting close too quickly and not sustaining the relationship. This can become a relational pattern for individuals who have not been able to develop their identities. Erikson holds that it is "only after a reasonable sense of identity has been established that real intimacy with the other sex (and for that matter with any other person...) is possible" (1980, 101). Many continue to struggle with their identities and engage in unhealthy interpersonal relationships. Such people experienced abandonment, rejection, loneliness, and sexual abuse while growing up.

Erikson adds, "When a youth does not accomplish such intimate relations with others... with his own inner resources, in late adolescence or early adulthood he may either isolate himself... or seek them in repeated attempts and repeated failures" (Year, 1980,101). Oftentimes, religious sisters say that they are married to Christ or to the Church. How valid is this statement if one has not yet established her own identity as a person? One of the tasks in young adulthood is to develop the ability to see "someone else's needs and concerns as equally important as one's own" (Colarusso 1992). Becoming a parent sets the stage for "the establishment of an inner sense of equality and mutuality with his or her parents" (Colarusso 1992, 141). Such people struggle to hold onto a sense of self and even trust that self. Work productivity becomes a source of frustration or a necessary evil. A sense of isolation and eprivation attacks those for whom this rich period is not realized. The aging religious sister or nun may no doubt feel very isolated and left out if life has not brought her such riches to remember and relish.

To support this point, Winnicott talked about the "capacity to use others and to be used" (1968). This has to do with our being able to enjoy another person and have the experience of being enjoyed by others. To be able to use another, we must have had the opportunity to develop a capacity to use others. This is not abuse; rather it is the ability to enter an authentic relationship with someone else. According to Winnicott, "to use an object the subject must have developed a capacity to use objects.... The capacity cannot be said to be inborn nor can its development in an individual be taken for granted. The development of a capacity to use an object is another example of the maturational process as something that depends on a facilitating environment" (1968, 119-120). It is "the ability to enter deeply into authentic relationship whether with self (or) others" (Hamman 2014, 145). Winnicott used the terms *object relating* and *object usage* (Winnicott 1982, 117). He states, "First there is object-relating then in the end there is object-use" (1982, 120). He reminds us that object usage is the next developmental step in human relating, once a person has mastered object relating. His definition of *object relating* involves "joining to... one's inner world, in which the subject relates to the object through defenses like projective-identification.

However, object usage involves the subjective viewing and relating to the object outside of his own inner world, as a 'thing' in itself" (Winnicott 1989, 221-222). There are two ways we engage. "In object relating we internalize the relationships. In the process of relating to our care givers we internalize whatever goes on. Object usage occurs when one sees the object as it is real, after the object has survived the attacks of being used" (Winnicott 1982, 120). During the object usage phase, the infant will gradually and progressively become aware of the object's independent existence; the object's survival of the infant's destructive attacks show the infant the limits of its power and fosters a greater recognition in the infant of what is inside and what is outside. In his book *The Maturation Process and the Facilitating Environment,* Winnicott states, "The physical holding, cuddling, and the ordinary maternal preoccupation are some of the ways a mother can show her infant that she loves her. Being cuddled and rocked and held is experienced by the child as love.... Good-enough mothering cannot be accomplished by following a set of rules; instead, the mother understands her infant's needs based on empathy" (1968, 48-51). If a child had no opportunity to experience the joy of being held and cuddled and rocked and seen and treated as unwanted the end result will be isolation and loss of identity in her growing up. Hamman explains that "healthy emotional... development then is seen in the capacity to discover and use another person and in allowing others to use you. This capacity requires good enough parenting and a facilitating environment. It takes a mother, a father or a caregiver who survived the ruthlessness of the care for the child to assure usage" (2014, 153). Crucially, Winnicott believes that this capacity to use objects and be used is a capacity that develops through the holding phase and that failure in maternal provision in these phases can lead to the infant's not adequately recognizing the object as an external phenomenon and, as a result, having late psychopathology.

### *Generative vs. Stagnation: Care in Adulthood*

When a child is not seen or noticed by the mother, since the mother's face or eyes is the first mirror of the infant, the child may see only herself because her mother's face is unresponsive (Winnicott 1971, 1982). If a child's emotional needs were stunted by caregivers because a mother's face was unresponsive, then the child will lack approval from the mother and the child's healthy emotional development will be affected. There will be stagnation in the growth of this individual. This is an emotional pain, as expressed by a patient:

*I left my mother's home at a young age. I could not cope anymore. I teamed upwith my friend D. We did awful things. We drank together, smoked together, and changed men together. Oh! It is horrible looking back. I had no control over my life; my life was a mess. Can you believe this? I traveled to habitat with my friend D. I do not remember how we arrived there, if it was by air, sea, or land. This is to show you how drunk we were. I had a stunted childhood and adolescent life. I worked and got a few dollars, and with it I found a habitat to live my life. I say I am sober. I have not used alcohol, but I use cigars, nicotine, and weed. I visit my friend D as an excuse to smoke weed. I do not want to sabotage my journey of recovery. If I drink again I will be in despair. I need to go to AA meetings. Please help me. I was imagining what could happen if I drank again. Maybe I will lose my job, my apartment, or my mind and then I will die.*

The patient exhibited inner pain and frustration. She had imagined the terror of the then little girl of six until her teenage years, when she was subjected to inhumane treatment of pain and abuse by her own mother, being sexually violated, not knowing whom to tell, being transported from one home to another, and all without knowing who her father was. One could only feel compassion and empathy for this patient. Owing to the harsh treatment this patient had endured from her mother, she was unable to achieve Erikson's stages of trust and mistrust as well as autonomy versus shame and doubt. Instead, she had internalized mistrust and shame and doubt. Her shame was a shame of not being accepted or loved. She felt defeated and had experienced extreme shame and doubt growing up; she engaged in neurotic attempts to regain feelings of control, power, and competence. This had taken the form of indulging in obsessive behaviors for a long period. She had tried to repress the traumatic experiences she had endured growing up in her own way.

Nancy McWilliams, in her book *Psychoanalytical Diagnosis: Understanding Personality Structure in the Clinical Process*, says, "Repression is motivated forgetting or ignoring" (1994, 118). It is one of the secondary defenses, or higher-order defenses. She quotes Freud regarding the purpose of repression: "The essence of repression lies simply in turning something away, and keeping it at a distance, from the conscious." (1994, 118). She adds, "Only when there is evidence that an idea or emotion or perception has become consciously inaccessible because of its power to upset are there grounds for assuming the operation of this defense" (118).

Bradshaw comments, "As the shame develops, the child stops trusting his own eyes, judgment and feelings and desires" (2005, 101). He adds, "When caretakers are untrustworthy, children develop a deep sense of distrust. The world seems a dangerous, hostile, unpredictable place. So, the child must always be on guard and in control. He comes to believe, 'If I control everything, then no one can catch me off guard'"" (Bradshaw 1990, 13).

### *Generativity vs. Stagnation: Seventh Stage*

The seventh stage of Erikson's psychosocial development is generativity versus stagnation. In adulthood, syntonic (harmonious) and generative go hand in hand. Those who move successfully from the sixth stage, intimacy versus isolation, have a circle of friends and family who can bring them joy to navigate the seventh stage. They feel satisfied and proud. If they did not navigate stage six successfully, they feel embarrassed and incomplete, making the seventh stage harder for them, and the idea of leaving a legacy becomes a problem. Generativity is centered on reaching out and contributing to the next generation. It is about making a mark. It is concerned with establishing and guiding the next generation through the procreation of children.

*Generativity* is defined as "the generation of new beings as well as new products and new ideas" (Erikson 1982, 67). The new ideas will be needed to create a better world. The opposite of generativity is stagnation, self- absorption, or self-centeredness. Such people have no interest in productivity, and they place their concerns above everyone else's (Feist and Feist, 2009). "The generational cycle of productivity and creativity is crippled when people are too self-absorbed in themselves, too self-indulgent" (Feist and Feist 2009, 261*). Stagnation* refers to the failure to find a way to contribute to the next generation. These individuals must have felt disconnected from their community and society at large. Stagnation indicates no effort to improve and failure to get involved with others or activities. According to Erikson, "The principal thing is to realize that at this stage of the growth of the healthy personality ... where such enrichment fails... regression from generativity to an obsessive need for pseudo intimacy takes place" (1980, 103). When this stage is achieved, the basic strength is care. Erikson defines care "as widening commitment to take care of persons, the products, and the ideas one has learned to care for" (1982, 67). "As the basic strength of adulthood, care arises from each earlier basic ego strength. One must have hope, will, purpose, competence, fidelity, and love in order to take care of that which one cares for. Care is not a duty or obligation but a natural desire emerging from the conflict between generativity and stagnation or self-absorption" (Feist and Feist 2009, 261). The opposite of *generativity* is *rejectivity,* and this is a core pathology in adulthood. Rejectivity is the unwillingness to take care of a certain person or group (Erikson 1982). Feist and Feist explained, "Rejectivity is manifested as self-centeredness, provincialism, or pseudospeciation: that is, the belief that other groups of people are inferior to one's own. It is responsible for much of human hatred, destruction, atrocities and wars" (2009, 261). Erikson confirmed this, saying, "Rejectivity has far-reaching implications for the survival of the species as well as for every individual's psychosocial development" (Erikson 1982, 70). Winnicott's capacity for concern is very appropriate at this time of generativity and stagnation. The individual with the capacity for concern will be moved naturally to care for others and be creative in doing so.

**Integrity vs. Despair: Wisdom in Old Age**

The old-age stage (sixty-five years to death) is the eighth and final stage of Erikson's psychosocial development. At this stage, one would wonder if one has lived a meaningful life. Many older and sickly religious women reach this point in their lives with lots of regret and sorrow. Those who are unsuccessful during this phase will feel that their lives have been wasted and will experience many regrets. These individuals will face feelings of bitterness and despair. "Despair," Erikson says, "is a feeling that the time is now short, too short for the attempt to start another life and to try out alternatives roads" (1963, 266). The psychosocial crisis of this stage is integrity versus despair, and the basic strength of this stage is wisdom. Erikson defines wisdom as "informed and detached concern with life itself in the face of death itself" (1982, 61). He adds that the opposite of wisdom is Disdain, which he defines as "a reaction to feeling (and seeing others) in an increasing state of being finished, confused, helpless" (Erikson 1982, 61). Feist and Feist explain that for "people with a strong ego identity who have learned intimacy and who have taken care of both people and things, the syntonic quality of integrity will predominate" (2009, 262). They add, "Integrity means a feeling of wholeness and coherence, an ability to hold together one's sense of 'I-ness' despite diminishing physical and intellectual power" (Feist and Feist 2009, 262). Erikson believes that his developmental stages are appropriate to nearly all cultures past and present (Feist and Feist 2009). For Erikson, ego integrity "implies an emotional integration which permits participation by fellowship as well as acceptance of the responsibility of leadership: both must be learned and practiced in religion and politics, in the economic order" (1994, 105). He laments, "Society does not truly know how to integrate elders into its primary patterns and conventions or into its vital functioning.... Aged individuals are often... overlooked... seen no longer as bearers of wisdom" (Erikson 1997, X).

Berryman states, "Play makes us young when we are old" (1991, 1). Therefore, whether we are young or old, we need to look for a way to imagine and then play. We adults need to reclaim the playfulness we had experienced; playfulness keeps us alive because it is exciting and healthy (see Winnicott, capacity to imagine and to play).

**Trauma and the Sequalae in the Growth Development of the Individual**

A good number of the individuals who join the religious life lived through childhoods that were dominated by cumulative traumas: the trauma of not being wanted during pregnancy, of losing a parent and being reared or raised by someone else, of being rejected and abandoned by the biological father, and of physical and emotional abuse. Others come from dysfunctional homes, homes dominated by extreme poverty, or low-income families, which causes them to have very low self- esteem. This brings them shame. Shame is one of the traumas a child can experience in her developmental process. Bradshaw writes,

*When shame is toxic, it is an excruciatingly internal experience of unexpected exposure. It is a deep cut felt primarily from inside. It divides us from ourselves and from others. When our feeling of shame becomes toxic shame, we disown ourselves.*

*And this disowning demands a cover-up. It loves darkness and secretiveness. (2005, 5)*

"As the shame develops the child stops trusting his own eyes, judgments, feelings and desires" (Bradshaw 2005, 101). When a child is shamed to the extent where she cannot bear it any longer, she disowns and separates from this part of herself. This is called dissociation, an unconscious defense mechanism in which threatening ideas or feelings are kept from the rest of the psyche. Ira Brenner coined the term dissociative self and described it as, "This experience is not happening 'to me' it may be "somebody else" (2001, xi-xii). Kalsched states, "Dissociation is a normal part of the psyche's defense against trauma's potentially damaging impact." He continues, "Dissociation is a trick the psyche plays on itself. It allows life to go on by dividing up the unbearable experiences" and distributing them to the different compartments of the mind and body, especially the unconscious' aspects of the mind and body" (1996, 13). Sometimes, effects and images may be split from the conscious aspect of knowledge.

According to Babette Rothschild, a member of the International and European Society for Traumatic Stress Studies, "Shame is expected to be a component of PTSD when the trauma is the result of sexual abuse or rape" (2000, 62). Who knows what has gone on in the world of the individual who chooses to

become a religious sister since some of these issues might not be known even to the people who suffered them? Judith Herman discusses traumatic disorders and disconnection in her book *Trauma and Recovery*. She makes two very important points:

1. "Traumatized people who cannot spontaneously dissociate may attempt to produce similar numbing effects by using alcohol."

2. "Traumatic events call into question basic human relationships. They breach attachments of family, friendship, love and community. They shatter the construction of the self that is formed and sustained in relation to others." (Herman 1997, 44-51)

According to the *APA Dictionary of Psychology*, "Any conscious and unconscious adjustment or adaptation that decreases tension and anxiety in a stressful experience or situation" (2007 232) is a coping mechanism. But whether the coping mechanism is a positive or negative one is another matter. Individuals who choose to become sisters or nuns may have all kinds of maladaptive coping mechanisms. In Winnicott's concept of a healthy individual, he states, "There are those who did suffer traumatic experience of the kind that results from environmental let-down, and who must carry with them all their lives the memories" (1986, 31). For Winnicott, there is hope in delinquent behavior: "Often the child feels mad because of having a compulsion to do something without knowing why" (1986, 93). In other words, these behaviors are a cry for help.

Norman Wright, a trauma counselor, states, "Trauma is a wound. It is a wound in the brain" (2001, 197). He adds, "Trauma is a thief. It steals from a person. Trauma takes away their sense of wellbeing, security, predictability and safety" (Wright 2001, 231). Kalsched, in his book The Inner World of Trauma, states, "For the person who has suffered unbearable pain the psychological defense of dissociation allows external life to go on but at great internal cost. The outer trauma ends, and its effect may be largely 'forgotten' but the psychological sequelae of the trauma continue to haunt the inner world" (1996, 13). He defines trauma as "any experience that causes the child unbearable psychic pain or anxiety.... It varies from the acute experiences of child abuse to the more cumulative trauma of unmet needs" (Kalsched 1996, 1). When a child's life has been dominated by trauma, the child protects herself through dissociation. Winnicott believes that "trauma involves a consideration of external factors" (1989, 145), for it starts early. He affirms, "At the start trauma implies a breakdown in the area of reliability in the 'average expectable environment,' at the stage of near-absolute dependence" (Winnicott 1989, 145). He adds, "The result of such breakdown shows in the failure... in the establishment of personality structure and ego organization" (Winnicott 1989, 145). Miller adds, "The earliest traumas cannot consciously be recalled but are manifested in destructive and self- destructive behavior" (1984, 117). Cori writes, "Shame is one of the most painful emotions anyone can feel. It is the sense of being fundamentally flawed, wrong or bad. It is like a mother telling a child, "You can't count on me" (2010, 108).

Hamman explains that shame is the painful feeling of being exposed, being made vulnerable, being uncovered and left unprotected, or being naked and being looked at by others. Shame is the result of experiencing the ruthlessness of someone and seeing that the act of reparation rarely comes (2014, 104). He continues, "Shame is a dynamic that keeps us from flourishing... and is often a source of our destructiveness" (Hamman 2014, 104). If growing children are made to feel unloved, unwanted, and like a mistake, they grow up with a sense of feeling stuck, defeated, and hopeless. Shame may lead them to use substances to self-sooth, a condition that sometimes becomes difficult to treat. Cori adds, "Addiction is a common response to pain..........It is related to not being able to self-soothe and regulate one's emotions. Unable to process these uncomfortable emotions... the person engages in addictive behaviors" (2010, 115). "Shame is internalized when a child feels abandoned. Abandonment... describes how one loses one's authentic self and ceases to exist psychologically. Children cannot be who they are without a reflection mirror" (Bradshaw 2005, 31).

To buttress this point, McNish adds, "Shame... is an essential failure of trust in the goodness of oneself and others, and ultimately it is distrust in the goodness of God and life, distrust that we are the apple of God's eye, distrust that God is with us in the midst of suffering and adversity. Shame may be seen as a failure to trust in the essential acceptance and lovingness of life itself. In short shame is a failure of the experience of grace. It is a godless place" (2004, 36). A young adult asked the researcher this question: "Where was God when I was sent to the group home? Where was he when I was being molested because my mother was on drugs and could not care for me? Where was God when I came back from church and found my mom dead in the bathtub owing to drug overdose?" This young adult had not felt God's presence in her shame. When we understand our shame and refuse to use our shame defenses, we can experience a new level of emotional and relational maturity.

According to Wright, a trauma expert, in his book Crisis and Trauma Counseling, "Children of divorced parents are more likely to drop out of school. They tend to carry a pattern of insecurity, depression, anxiety into their adult years because of the extent of the loss" (2011, 335). One theorist commented on this: "Although they come to therapy out of need, they do not really want to grow or change in ways that would truly satisfy that need.... One part of them wanted to change and a stronger part resisted this change. They were divided within themselves" (Kalsched 1996, 11). Kalsched notes further,

All of them had become prematurely self-sufficient in their childhood, cutting off genuine relations with their parents during their developing years and caretaking themselves in a cocoon of fantasy instead. They tended to see themselves as the victims of others' aggression and could not mobilize effective self-assertion when it was needed to defend themselves or to individuate. Their outward façade of toughness and self-sufficiency often concealed a secret dependency they were ashamed of.... They found it very difficult to relinquish their own self-care protection and allow themselves to depend on a real person. (Kalsched 1996, 12)

Forward adds that a mother who is unable to teach her daughter to navigate life is not good enough (2014). If a mother is not available to cook meals, take care of her child or children, or even look after herself—it does not matter if she is depressed, alcoholic, addicted, or infantile-it seems she will need more mothering herself than she can give. In this scenario, her daughter will find herself taking on the role of the parents or mother, protector, and even the confidante of the mother.

Fairbairn states that repression of one's bad object is related to shame. He explains that, because a child's object relationships are built on identification, if his objects are bad, then he also feels bad; that is, he thinks he is also bad. Fairbairn reminds us that everyone has some internalized bad objects. He states, "It is impossible for anyone to pass through childhood without having bad objects which are internalized and repressed. Hence internalized bad objects are present in the minds of all of us at a deeper level" (Fairbairn 1994, 64-65). Regarding the splitting of the ego, Fairbairn envisions the child with largely unavailable parents as differentiating between the responsive aspects of the parents (the good) and the unresponsive aspects (the bad).

Fairbairn also observed that "the relationship with bad objects is experienced by the child not only as painful but also shameful" (1994, 63). When a child grows up without the satisfactory emotional support of a nurturing object or caretaker, bad internal objects are formed. Fairbairn described three main categories of internal objects. One is in the conscious part of the self, and the other two are repressed in the unconscious (Scharff and Scharff 1997, 21). This child grows up feeling that she cannot be loved and valued for who she is and that her own love will not be appreciated and valued. These children grow up and "scramble for love, care and attention wherever they can find it, and once having found it, cling to it with a desperation that leads them to unloving manipulative, Machiavellian behavior that destroys the very relationships they seek" (Peck 2003, 104). "A little girl who was criticized or ignored or abused or stifled by an unloving mother," says Forward, "becomes an adult who tells herself she'll never be good enough or lovable enough... or acceptable enough to deserve success and happiness because if you really were worthy of respect and affection, a voice inside whispers, your mother would have given them to you" (2014, 4). In all these, the role of perception should not be underestimated.

**Concept of Perception**

Perception as a psychological concept does not easily lend itself to a definition. "To perceive is to become aware directly through any of the senses, especially sight or hearing, to achieve understanding of" (American Heritage Collegiate Dictionary 1997, 1,013). Bartley sees perception as the immediate discriminatory response of the organism to energy-activating sense of organs (1969). The concept of perception is also seen by early psychologists Tagiuri and Petrullo as an act of perceiving in terms of basic data and sensory experiences (1958).

Wundt, an early psychologist, considers perception to be the immediate response of an organism to the impingement of energy upon one of its specialized sense organs, such as the eyes, ears, tongue, receptors in the nose, and the variety of receptors in the skin (1904). In the same way, Allport, in his attempt to define the concept of perception, states that perception can be defined as having something to do with the awareness of the object or conditions about us (1995). He goes on to explain that perception is dependent, to a large extent, on the impression these objects make on our senses. It is the way things look to us or the way they sound, feel, or smell. Brunner, Goodnow, and Austin give a new dimension to the study of perception. For them perception involves decision processes, a placement of incoming information into a network of meaningful categories developed largely from prior learning (Bruner et al. 1956). They conclude that perception refers to the ways that we understand our environment; an individual's environment and past experiences are important in her understanding and acceptance of a concept or event. The success or failure of certain events in the past can affect the individual's perception.

## Perceptual Factors that Influence Behavior

Perception, being more or less a cognitive process, can be influenced by many factors that can in turn affect behaviors. Huston et al. indicate that individuals' past experiences can influence their perceptions and hence their behavior (1989). They contend that limited knowledge can affect people's perceptions and cause them to behave in a particular manner. Therefore, religious sisters or nuns who have adequate knowledge about who they are and what they bring to the religious life will embrace it positively and look for ways and means of developing their capacities, while those with limited knowledge about themselves may see nothing wrong with their behaviors.

## Call to Religious Life

People join convents for all kinds of reasons. Even though it feels to them that they want to serve God, underneath this manifest content is something else of which they might not be conscious. When young ladies or women walk to the doors of the convent, they do not leave their spirituality in their homes.

They bring their spiritual beliefs, practices, values, and struggles along with them. What then is this spiritual life or spirituality? Spirituality is a broad concept. Generally, it includes a sense of connectedness to something bigger than oneself. It includes connectedness to us, and our fellow creatures. It also involves one's search for meaning in life. The term spirituality has its roots in Latin, Greek, and Hebrew. It means "wind," "air," or "breathe." It is that which gives life. The essence of a spiritual life is for all aspects of our selves to balance as we are body, mind, and soul; and all three have to be in harmony for us to function fully. When one's spiritual life is meaningful—that is, when one is meaningfully connected with something bigger or beyond oneself-and it ends in positive emotions, such as peace, contentment, gratitude and acceptance, it aids one's emotional well-being.

God always speaks to the hearts of individuals. He does call in a way that only the ears and heart of the person being called can hear. This type of call needs one who can understand the deep meaning of what is being said by the caller, who is God. This call to the religious life is a call to become conformed to Christ. To become like him is to have a Christlike character (Rom 1:7). The invitation of Christ is addressed to all who can follow the call, to "he who can take it." It is as if Christ is saying, I force no one but I invite everyone who can come (Mat 19:11-12) for the sake of the kingdom. It means not all can accept this invitation but let those who can accept. In Antioch, the people called followers of Christ "Christians" because they behaved like Christ (Acts 11:26). Like Levi the tax collector (Lk 5:29), to answer the call, one needs to leave everything and follow Jesus. In the gospels, when Jesus called his followers, they left everything-relatives, wealth, and security and followed (Mat 4:18-22). In the same vein, those who choose to answer this call will need to have trust in the one who called them. One who is called to the religious life will need to be attracted to spend time with Christ just as he, Christ, spent time with the Father. Trust is therefore a basic factor in choosing to enter the religious life (Erikson 1997; Winnicott 1960). An individual who is unable to achieve the first stage of Erikson's psychosocial stage of trust need not consider this life, for mistrust in all aspects will be a danger to the person and others. A person called to this life needs some appropriate emotional maturity because she will always need to think a situation through before making a choice. It is amid the tug and pull of personality and in the crucible of formation and reformation that the young woman chooses to explore the religious life, choosing to enter the religious life whether or not she has worked through the stages of maturity. If this individual enters without having adequately worked through those stages, if she lacks the six capacities enumerated by Winnicott, then the convent environment will be chaotic for her and others. If she has no capacity to believe, as Winnicott points out, I will be difficult for her to believe in God, the very being she seeks to serve. When she is unable to believe in something, she will lack trust-trust in herself, trust in people she will live with, trust in the structure of the daily activities, and trust in prayer itself. No one can live this life without prayer and contemplation, so this young woman without these capacities will not be able to live the life.

Similarly, lacking the capacity to believe in something will hinder a person from even trying to imagine things, thus losing the capacity to imagine at all. Without that capacity, this individual cannot play because, to be able to be playful with one self, with community members, and with those to whom she would minister, she needs to have the capacity to imagine how that playful activity will go. Therefore, the capacity to imagine and the capacity to play go hand in hand. Since playing sometimes involves a lack of compassion, the individual seeking this life needs the capacity for concern-concern for herself, for others, and for those to whom she would minister. Without the capacity for concern, she will trample upon others, take them for granted, and think her behavior is appropriate. Lack of this capacity will make reparation impossible since there will be a lack of empathy as well. One can only imagine the atmosphere in a religious community where a group of women living together lack the capacity for concern, empathy, and reparation. The next two capacities are essential: the capacity to be alone and the capacity to use and be used by others. Lacking the capacity to be alone means this individual will be clingy and fish for favors from people in authority, for comfort from other members, and for companionship from outsiders. What a burden for those living in the same environment with this person. Contemplation and silence, which this life requires, will be burdensome for this individual. Since she lacks the capacity to use others and be used, she will bully others and emotionally abuse them, sometimes through gossip, slander, and the like, without any qualms of conscience. If she lacks the capacity to use others and be used, she will also lack the maturity that goes with this capacity. It will, therefore, be a grave mistake for such an individual to join this way of life unless she is willing to work on her emotional and psychological maturity. The calling to the religious life requires a physical journey of moving from one's home to the convent, and it also requires a true inner journey. This journey of transformation must be taken if one desires wholeness.

Walt Whitman, the American poet, writes, "Not I, nor anyone else can travel that road for you. You must travel it by yourself. It is not far. It is within reach. Perhaps you have been on it since you were born, and did not know" (2007, 80). After the individual has made her decision (discerned) to answer the call, she chooses to visit some religious communities where their life attracts her desires or appeals to her (since there are many religious communities and each has its own character). This discernment takes time because it is a process that involves continual prayer and searching of heart. Some things will be certain: that this individual is seriously interested in a deep friendship with Jesus or God and that this relationship has been developing within this individual for a while. During the period of discernment, the individual chooses to visit the communities to learn more about them before considering joining them. There is no time limit on the discernment process. So much goes on in the person's inner world-for example, the ideas that she will never have her own children or use her money as she wants or pleases become a struggle for her. Once the discernment is done, the individual applies to join the specific society she has chosen. There are no certifications or licensing requirements to become a religious sister or nun.

**Consecrated Life or Religious Life**

Consecrated life is the total dedication of one's life to God. They assume the evangelical counsels and become members of a particular institute according to the laws of the church (Code of Canon Law section 573.2). Religious life is a "following of Christ" (Pc 2a) and "a sharing in the life of the church" (Pc 2c). Choosing to become a religious woman is embracing an invitation to enter into the depth of oneself. A desire to become a religious woman is about seeking a personal transformation before one ministers to others. It looks as though an individual may have an idea of what the religious life is about, but she does not perceive the depth. Choosing this way of life means one is prepared to mature into an authentic person who can interact with others in a whole, holistic manner-an emotional, spiritual, physical, and psychological manner. If the lack of the capacities mentioned earlier is not taken into consideration, the end result is always an influx of people in the convents who choose to be friendly with those with whom they want to be friendly, especially those in authority; go through the stages of formation; and once they are out or are finally professed, these behaviors manifest.

In all of us there is a sacred garden "where the soul" abides, where the "transcendent reality" lives (Pargament 2011, 32). The human person's first spiritual and physical home was the garden of Eden. In the garden, which was literally paradise (Gen 2:1:16), Adam and Eve had plenty to eat and time to commune with God and be companions to each other. In the garden, or home, they were at peace physically and psychologically. Spiritually and psychologically, they were in tune with God. They were able to communicate with God. They were able to be alone in the presence of God without any hindrance. Before the fall, there was order, not chaos. After the fall, chaos and inner turmoil manifested. Adam and Eve had to move out of the presence of God. In this garden, where "ideas of God, higher powers, divinity or the ultimate reality lies," is what Pargament again calls "the sacred core" (Pargament 2011, 32). When we are able to reach this core, life begins to make sense to us. Reaching this core means openness to our own selves and others (Winnicott's capacity to imagine and play). Before the fall, they were naked but not ashamed (Gen 2:25). Choosing to be what they were not resulted in suffering. Their problem, nakedness, prevented them from being alone with God.

This time, they hid from God when theyheard his voice. Tillich calls the dramatic exit of paradise and its repercussions "psychic disruption in man, ... the disintegration of man" (1984, 18-19). We are made to be connected to God, and so, as Augustine says, "Our hearts are restless until they rest in you" (Augustine 1955, 31). Traveling to reach the core is a journey. Herman Hesse said this of the journey: "Journeys are a great experience. I was permitted to be a participant in the unique journey ... but in the difficult years of misfortune, sickness and deep affliction... no allurement or threat in the world would induce me to break my vow" (1968, 4-5). He adds, "Our goal was not only to the east... it was the home... of the soul" (1968, 27).

Religious women are also made in the image and likeness of God. They are to be connected to God and to their core. It so happens that individuals in the religious communities choose to be out of tune with God. Lacking the capacities that Winnicott enumerated, failing to navigate Erikson's eight psychosocial stages, and manifesting these problematic behaviors means these individuals are unable to reach the core Pargament talked about. Because they chose to be what they are not, their hearts will be restless until they rest in God (Augustine 1955). Having a restless heart means not being in tune with God and, therefore, being unable to function properly. For some, the religious life does not make sense; for others, it is cumbersome. This is all because the connectedness with their core is off balance. Shame prevents people from progressing and doing what is right and fitting. If these behaviors are unrestricted, they will be out of tune with God, and this can affect all aspect of the religious life-from prayer life to ministries sisters engage in. It becomes human filled instead of God filled, echoing the words of Tillich: "psychic disruption in man ... disintegration of man" (1984, 18-19).

A religious life is a consecrated life by which the faithful are called to follow Jesus Christ in a more exacting way, including the public profession of poverty, chastity, and obedience, which is also called the evangelical counsels (Code of Canon Law section 573, 1983). It is a free response to the invitation of the Holy Spirit to follow Christ more closely. The duty of a religious sister or nun depends on her religious society. It could be teaching, nursing, or catechesis. Nuns of each society identify themselves with a specific dress and most often live in communities or alone (secular institutes). There are three main stages in the religious life, which are called the formative years.

**Stages of the Religious Formation Process**

These stages are the phases of discernment as women advance toward making a lifelong commitment to a religious community. The first formation period is called candidacy. It lasts from six months to one year. The person gets to know the community members and is called an aspirant or candidate. She lives outside the community and visits for "Am I Called?" or "Come and See" programs. These programs assist the individual in making her decision.

The next stage is postulancy, in which the individual is called a postulant. This stage takes one to two years, during which the individual lives with the members of the community, learning their way of life.

The third stage is the novitiate, during which the individual is called a novice and addressed as "sister." This stage lasts two years. There are rituals that go with each stage, and these differ from community to community. The first of the two years is called a canonical year and is dedicated to prayer. The individual explores the meaning of the vows and learns about the religious life as well as the religious congregation of which she has decided to become part. The second year of the two years is for ministry of the society.

The fourth stage is the temporal profession of vows, in which the individual who is now called a sister makes a public profession of the vows of poverty, chastity, and obedience. It takes one to six years. At the end of these six years, the sister professes her final or perpetual vows, becoming a finally professed sister. This stage used to last nine years but has been reduced to six. The nun or sister devotes herself to a life of poverty and simplicity. Some collect a salary if they work as teachers or doctors. The daily needs of nuns, such as housing and food, are provided for by their religious communities. Once the final vows are taken, the sisters are expected to spend their entire lives devoted to their faith, to the study of the teachings of the church, and to other studies. Some become leaders in the societies, while others become novices, postulants, and temporal professed mistresses or directors.

A religious sister is a member of a religious community of women who lives under vows of poverty, chastity, and obedience. She may choose to dedicate her life to serving others in an active order, that is, working in the mainstream of society, or she may choose to be an ascetic, one who voluntarily chooses to leave the mainstream society and live a contemplative life in a convent, abbey, or monastery (Wikipedia 2021).

**Basic Requirements for Entering**

In my own experience and in the experiences of others, the basic requirements for entering are generally as follow:

**1. True vocation from a supernatural motive**

One must have genuine desire that stems from God; in other words, the attraction must be worthwhile.

**2. Good health**

It is important that the aspiring sister or nun be physically and psychologically able to engage in the work of the apostolate and the mission of the congregation. Healthy is a broad term, so the vocational personnel are always there for such discussions.

**3. Aptitude for the life and work of the congregation**

The individual choosing to join this congregation must have the capacity to engage in the daily activities of the congregation.

## 4. Must be a Catholic woman

If the person is not a Catholic, she can look for other forms of religious life or Christian communities that are not exclusively Catholic (Anglican nuns) or other traditions (Buddhist nuns). To be a Catholic nun, the person will need to be baptized by a Catholic priest before beginning.

## 5. Must be single

The person must currently not be married in the eyes of the Church. In some religious congregations, widows may be validly accepted.

## 6. Must be eighteen to twenty-five years old

This is the normal age range in most relatively new congregations. The range is extended for older and less populated congregations.

## 7. Other considerations

Most religious congregations like mine require some form of education, but one must have a high school or college degree before entering. However, professional experience is not necessarily a requirement.

If these broad requirements are not understood fully by this individual seeking to enter, what is missing? In some orders, nothing is done with regard to this "good health" that is specified in the requirements.

An individual preparing and choosing such an enterprise needs to be psychologically ready to uphold the evangelical vows of poverty, obedience, and chastity and, above all, ready to assume the community living of the chosen order. For this reason, this research becomes vital.

*Chapter 3*

# Research Methodology

This chapter describes the research design of the study, the population, the sampling technique used in the study, and the instrument used in the data collection.

**Research Hypotheses**

The researcher developed a method to help her address some of the unacceptable behavior patterns of religious women dedicated to the service of God so that they and others could have fulfillment in the lives they have chosen for themselves. The literature review assisted the researcher in concluding that certain environmental factors in an individual's growth processes play an important role in the behavior patterns that are most often observed by others in the day-to-day interactions in the convents. The researcher focuses on the fact that these behavior patterns and their understanding need to be brought to the consciousness of others so that life may be more livable for those living in the same space. The researcher makes the following argumentative hypotheses:

1. Children raised in unstable homes without proper care and nurturing love tend to suffer chronic emotional insufficiency in their adult lives even when they choose to live a religious life.

2. Unless an individual has a secure base while growing up with an intuitive and understanding caregiver, that individual is likely to face emotional turmoil as an adult.

3. Building a strong inner world with proper emotional balance from childhood on is crucial to coping with life in a healthy manner as an adult.

4. Steady emotional growth in different stages of life parallel to physical growth contributes to the evolving of a mature person who has the capacity to make the right choices and decisions.

5. Positive validation is very important in the growth of a child as she builds a stronger self within that reflects later in life as an adult with a healthy self- esteem.

6. In the choice of becoming a sister, an individual needs to possess a good, mature psychological framework, within which is the key to live a happy and joyful religious life.

7. A father's lack of emotional support for his growing child will make the child feel abandoned throughout her life.

**Research Design**

The researcher tried to describe and analyze Winnicott's capacities and Erikson's stages of developmental growth. The researcher used the sample-survey method. The research is non-experimental because it studies the relationship between non-manipulated variables in a natural setting. As Gay puts it, "The descriptive sample survey involves collecting data in order to test hypotheses or answer questions concerning the subject under study" (1987, 187). The descriptive sample survey is recommended by Babbie (1990) for the purpose of generalizing from a sample to a population so that inferences can be made about the characteristics, attributes, or behaviors of the population. Since it was the purpose of the research to assess what makes for a "good" religious sister (nun) through the "eyes" of Winnicott and Erikson, the research focuses on the careful observation of individuals' psychological lives by checking for behaviors manifesting in the religious communities. As the spiritual life is already taken care of by others, the intent here is to glean from these what patterns endure.

## The Population

It is worthwhile to say a little about the researcher's religious congregation. It is an international congregation, meaning that it comprises people with different cultural backgrounds. Such differences in culture have great influence on the general membership in the order. It is an undeniable fact that individuals from different cultural backgrounds join this society with different worldviews and behaviors. The population is made up of religious sisters from the different chosen orders. The total number of sisters chosen is two hundred. Sisters were chosen from five congregations of both diocesan and international orders.

## Sampling and Sampling Technique

The sampling technique adopted was simple random sampling. The sample for the study was made up of finally professed sisters, postulants, novices, and temporally professed sisters. In all, two hundred respondents were randomly selected.

## Instrument of Data Collection

The instrument that was used for the data collection was a questionnaire developed by the researcher, as well as interviews. The questions were chosen to elicit responses from the participants that will shed light on the topic under study. Group process was also used by the researcher.

## Pretesting or Refining the Instrument

The draft questionnaire was submitted to the researcher's supervisor for his suggestions and revisions. Some refinements were made based on his comments, suggestions, and criticisms. To make sure that respondents understood the questionnaire, the instrument was pretested with three postulants, five novices, five finally professed sisters, and five temporally professed sisters in an order different from those selected for the study. The selected participants were asked to fill out the questionnaire and provide their comments and suggestions. The researcher went through all the items carefully and noted words that needed to be changed. All corrections, comments, and suggestions from the participants were taken into consideration in the final version of the instrument.

## Reliability of the Instrument

The researcher concluded that consistency across the board of data gathering was paramount. In every case, the freedom and independence of the participants to make their choices on items was maintained. Against this backdrop, the data will prove trustworthy.

## Data-Collection Procedure

The researcher herself distributed the questionnaire to the participants. In administering the questionnaire, the researcher contacted the leaders of the religious orders and explained to them the purpose and significance of the study and entreated them to complete the questionnaire in a week. It took the researcher a couple of months to retrieve the questionnaires.

As soon as the questionnaires were retrieved, thorough screening was done to identify missing information. Some of the respondents did not provide the information needed even though the questionnaires had been explained to them. Some of the congregation leaders refused to allow their sisters to take part in the research, claiming that "it will not be good for them" (sisters). Other sisters were afraid to let their "emotions out," as some sisters commented. Others wept upon scanning the questionnaire. As a result, the researcher conducted interviews in small groups to fill in the missing information. This served as a complement to the questionnaire and provided the missing information. A case study was also added by the researcher, as well as group process.

## Data-Analysis Procedure

After the questionnaires were returned, the researcher rendered the data in table format. This made it easier to track the data by frequencies and percentages. Against this backdrop, the data were carefully analyzed and interpreted in response to the research questions. This study was designed to test the hypotheses developed earlier.

# *Chapter 4*

# Data Presentation and Analysis

The following is the analysis of the questionnaire that was given to two hundred respondents (sisters). The data was collected from responses from 178 respondents.

The two hundred respondents of sisters or nuns were from different religious groups or congregations. All in the group profess the same three evangelical counsels of poverty, chastity, and obedience. They all start their training as candidates or postulants, novices, and then temporal professed sisters before they are finally professed. The data was collected with responses from 178 respondents, as 22 questionnaires could not be retrieved. In all the religious congregations, candidates or postulants were not given the opportunity to take part in the survey. Either the groups had no postulants or the sister or nun in charge of the postulants chose not to give them the opportunity to participate. It is interesting to note that all the groups did have postulants, including the researcher's own religious order. The questionnaire says, "Tick level in the congregation: Final professed, temporal professed, novice, postulant." None of the respondents ticked "postulant."

The first part of the questionnaire was designed to explore respondents' experiences with their fathers when growing up in their home environments. It had sixteen items or statements regarding this experience. Respondents were asked to indicate whether they grew up with their fathers or not. If they did not, they were asked to proceed to the second part of the questionnaire. If they did, they were asked to tick the sixteen items that applied to their growing up.

Question: Did you grow up with your father? If NO, skip the questions. If YES, indicate which things you had experienced in the relationship you had with your father.

- My father supported and encouraged me to become a leader.
- My father was a positive role model for me.
- My father was affectionate and playful with me.
- My father spent time listening to me and having conversations with me.
- My father would show up at my school and community activities and performances.
- My father encouraged me to do good at whatever I was doing.
- My father publicly rebuked or shamed me when I made mistakes.
- My father punished me when I made mistakes.
- My father encouraged me to do better when I made mistakes or fell short. •My father prevented or discouraged me from doing or pursing things I liked.
- My father was present in the home but did not interact positively with me. My father drove fear into me.
- My father did not show me that he loved me.
- My father tried to control what I did and how I did it.
- My father made me feel inadequate or not good enough.
- My father physically abused me.

|  | Number | Percent |
|---|---|---|
| Grew up in the same environment with father | 149 | 83.71% |
| Did not grow up in the same environment with page | 29 | 16.29% |

Out of the 178 responses received, 29 (16.29%) respondents indicated that they did not grow up with their fathers, and 149 (83.71%) indicated that they did grow up with their fathers.

We will proceed to analyze the other responses of those who did not grow up with their fathers and their responses to the second part of the questionnaire. The second part listed 59 behaviors in 6 columns, and respondents were to tick which behaviors they had observed in their various congregations; among the finally and temporally professed sisters, novices, and postulants or candidates; and their own behaviors in the convent environment. The number of finally professed sisters who took part in the survey was 118. The lengths of time they had been religious sisters ranged from seven years to fifty years. The temporally professed sisters, who had been in the religious life from four to six years, numbered thirty-two. This gap reflects that many more older sisters responded than younger ones because not many young people choose to join convents these days. Twenty- eight novices responded and had joined two to three years earlier.

| Behavior | Congregation | | Final Professed | | Temporal Professed | | Novices | | Postulants | | My Own | |
|---|---|---|---|---|---|---|---|---|---|---|---|---|
| | # | % | # | % | # | % | # | % | # | % | # | % |
| Untrusting | 13 | 44.83 | 11 | 39.93 | 19 | 65.52 | 15 | 51.72 | 13 | 44.83 | 10 | 34.48 |
| Difficulty in making and keeping friends | 12 | 41.38 | 4 | 13.79 | 16 | 55.17 | 15 | 51.72 | 14 | 48.28 | 13 | 44.83 |
| Tends to be angry most of the time | 10 | 34.48 | 7 | 24.14 | 16 | 55.17 | 12 | 41.38 | 11 | 37.93 | 6 | 20.69 |
| Tends to be needy | 13 | 44.83 | 10 | 34.48 | 20 | 68.97 | 22 | 75.86 | 24 | 82.76 | 11 | 37.93 |
| Tends to be overly defensive | 5 | 17.24 | 11 | 37.93 | 10 | 34.48 | 6 | 20.69 | 12 | 41.38 | 10 | 43.48 |
| Recognition seeking | 12 | 41.38 | 13 | 44.83 | 21 | 72.41 | 20 | 68.97 | 16 | 55.17 | 13 | 44.83 |
| Self-blaming | 7 | 24.14 | 12 | 41.38 | 9 | 31.03 | 13 | 44.83 | 16 | 55.17 | 11 | 37.93 |
| Anxious | 13 | 44.83 | 10 | 34.48 | 21 | 72.41 | 13 | 44.83 | 13 | 44.83 | 8 | 27.59 |
| Low self-esteem | 9 | 31.03 | 7 | 24.14 | 12 | 41.38 | 9 | 31.03 | 15 | 51.72 | 6 | 20.69 |
| Feelings of being ridiculed | 5 | 17.24 | 7 | 24.14 | 3 | 10.34 | 12 | 41.38 | 11 | 37.93 | 11 | 37.93 |
| Tends to get into other people's stuff | 14 | 48.28 | 13 | 44.83 | 8 | 27.59 | 10 | 34.48 | - | - | 9 | 31.03 |
| Discipline or retaliating by shaming | 11 | 37.93 | 7 | 24.14 | 11 | 37.93 | 7 | 24.14 | 4 | 13.79 | 10 | 34.48 |
| Feelings of loneliness | 8 | 27.59 | 2 | 6.90 | 12 | 41.38 | 13 | 44.83 | 19 | 65.52 | 7 | 24.14 |
| Fear of being judged | 1 | 3.45 | 2 | 6.90 | 19 | 65.52 | 17 | 58.62 | 8 | 27.59 | 7 | 24.14 |
| Feelings of worthlessness | 5 | 17.24 | 8 | 27.58 | 14 | 48.28 | 10 | 34.48 | 9 | 31.03 | 6 | 20.69 |

| Behavior | Congregation | | Final Professed | | Temporal Professed | | Novices | | Postulants | | My Own | |
|---|---|---|---|---|---|---|---|---|---|---|---|---|
| | # | % | # | % | # | % | # | % | # | % | # | % |
| Paranoid | 6 | 20.69 | 12 | 41.38 | 9 | 31.03 | - | - | 10 | 34.48 | 5 | 17.24 |
| Indecisive | 7 | 24.14 | 4 | 13.79 | 7 | 24.14 | 9 | 31.03 | 18 | 62.07 | 2 | 6.90 |
| Lacking coping skills | 12 | 41.38 | 7 | 24.14 | 7 | 24.14 | 12 | 41.38 | 12 | 41.38 | 9 | 31.03 |
| Suffer from mood swings | 13 | 44.83 | 9 | 31.03 | 10 | 34.48 | 10 | 34.48 | 9 | 31.03 | 11 | 37.93 |
| Trust issues | 15 | 51.72 | 13 | 44.83 | 21 | 72.41 | 16 | 55.17 | 17 | 58.62 | 12 | 41.38 |
| Crisis preoccupied | 6 | 20.69 | 6 | 20.69 | 5 | 17.24 | - | - | 12 | 41.38 | 2 | 6.90 |
| Unable to handle crises | 13 | 44.83 | 12 | 41.38 | 7 | 24.14 | 13 | 44.83 | 18 | 62.07 | 15 | 51.72 |
| Fear of being involved | 2 | 6.90 | 27 | 93.10 | 23 | 79.31 | 17 | 58.62 | 14 | 48.29 | 12 | 41.38 |
| Fear of rejection | 12 | 41.38 | 5 | 17.24 | 13 | 44.83 | 13 | 44.83 | 14 | 48.29 | 7 | 24.14 |
| Does not believe in oneself | 12 | 41.38 | 4 | 13.79 | 7 | 24.14 | 11 | 37.93 | 13 | 44.83 | 6 | 20.69 |
| Problem understanding | 11 | 37.93 | 5 | 17.24 | 7 | 24.14 | 13 | 44.83 | 9 | 31.03 | 5 | 17.24 |
| Lack of self-confidence | 8 | 27.59 | 6 | 20.69 | 18 | 62.07 | 2 | 6.90 | 12 | 41.38 | 6 | 20.69 |
| Emotionally inflexible | 3 | 10.34 | 8 | 27.59 | 10 | 34.48 | 5 | 17.24 | 12 | 41.38 | 10 | 34.48 |
| Routinely violates confidentiality | 5 | 17.24 | 3 | 10.34 | 12 | 41.38 | 7 | 24.14 | 12 | 41.38 | 6 | 20.69 |
| Difficulty envisioning a future (self) | 3 | 10.34 | 4 | 13.79 | 9 | 31.03 | 7 | 24.14 | 11 | 37.93 | 2 | 6.90 |
| Tends to be very aggressive | 5 | 17.24 | 6 | 30.68 | 16 | 55.17 | 10 | 34.48 | 15 | 51.72 | 5 | 17.24 |
| Gives up too easily | 5 | 17.24 | 2 | 6.90 | 5 | 17.24 | - | - | 8 | 27.59 | 6 | 30.68 |
| Too sensitive | 13 | 44.83 | 10 | 34.48 | 16 | 55.17 | 7 | 24.14 | 13 | 44.83 | 8 | 27.59 |
| Not interested in what others feel | 6 | 20.69 | 7 | 24.14 | 7 | 24.14 | 6 | 20.69 | 7 | 24.14 | 12 | 41.38 |
| Likes to fix other people's problems | 13 | 44.83 | 7 | 24.14 | 5 | 17.24 | - | - | 8 | 27.59 | 9 | 31.03 |
| Talks too much and listens too little | 15 | 51.72 | 15 | 51.72 | 9 | 31.03 | 10 | 34.48 | 7 | 24.14 | 12 | 41.38 |
| Inappropriate responses or behavior | 6 | 20.69 | 7 | 24.14 | 2 | 6.90 | 7 | 24.14 | 4 | 48.28 | 8 | 27.59 |

Table 2 lists the behaviors that were observed by the 29 respondents (16.29%) who did not grow up with their fathers. The data indicate that these behaviors observed among the congregations, finally professed, temporally professed, novices, postulants, and individuals do exist. The respondents indicated that most of the behaviors take place, even though the percentages vary. The behaviors that received the highest percentages of responses are "trust issues," "inability to control one's emotions," "talks too much and listens too little," "fear of being involved," and "tends to be needy." Even though only two respondents indicated they had witnessed the fear of being involved, their responses portray that there is such an issue. It is worth noting that temporal professed, novices, and postulants may not have responded to certain statements because they do not have much say in the congregation's overall affairs. Also, the tendency for congregations to panic in various situations is prevalent and evident in the "inability to handle emotions" responses. Molehill situations are always magnified; therefore, many respondents indicated that they have witnessed this issue. Other sisters ticked for them said they have witnessed many behaviors because they are beginners and most often find everything around them very confusing.

The behaviors that received the next- highest percentages of responses are "untrusting," "inability to control one's emotions," "talks too much and listens too little," "too sensitive," and "anxious." "Untrusting": congregations thirteen (44.83 %), Final professed eleven (37.93%), Temporal professed nineteen (65.52%), Novices fifteen (51.72%), Postulants thirteen (44.83%), and Own behavior ten (34.48%). "Inability to control one's emotions": Congregation fifteen (51.72%), Final professed eleven (37.93%), Temporal professed thirteen (44.83%), Novices fourteen (44.83%), Postulants eighteen (62.07%), Own behavior twelve (41.38%). "Talks too much and listens too little": Congregation fifteen (51.72%). "Too sensitive": Congregation thirteen (44.83%), Final professed ten (34.48 %), Temporal professed sixteen (55.17%), Novices seven (24.14%), Postulants thirteen (44.83%), and Own behavior eight (27.59%). "Anxious": Congregation thirteen (44.83%), Final professed ten (34.48%), Temporal professed twenty-one (72.41%), Novices thirteen(44.83%), Postulants thirteen (44.83%), and Own behavior eight (27.59%).

Agreement was equally high on the issues of recognition seeking, suffer from mood swings, and difficulty making and keeping friends. "Recognition seeking": Congregation twelve (41.38%), Final professed thirteen (44.83%), Temporal professed twenty- one (72.41 %), Novices twenty (68.97%), Postulants sixteen (55.17%), and Own behavior thirteen (44.83%). "Suffer from mood swings": Congregation thirteen (44.83%), Final professed nine (31.03%), Temporal professed ten (34.48%), Novices ten (34.48 %), Postulants nine (31.03%), and Own behavior eleven (37.93%). Interestingly, on the issue of "difficulty making and keeping friends," only four final professed (48.28%) ticked it, but many more in the other groups did. This brings us to the fact that these behaviors manifest among the sisters. The behavior "feelings of abandonment" was frequently witnessed by only sisters in temporal professed and postulants groups, with ten (34.48%) each.

Behaviors such as "low self-esteem," "emotionally distant," and "tends to get into other people's stuff" were all noticed by many among the different groups of respondents. Agreement was especially high on the behavior "tends to get into other people's stuff."

The data revealed that some behaviors were observed more by those in formation (temporal vows, novices, and postulants) than others: "untrusting," "difficulty making and keeping friends," "tends to be needy," "recognition seeking," "fear of being judged," "gets sad/depressed easily and often," "anxious," "trust issues," "feelings of abandonment," "lack of confidence," "self-blaming," "feelings of worthlessness," "indecisive," and "crisis preoccupied." "Untrusting: Temporal professed nineteen (65.52%), Novices fifteen (51.72%). Difficulty making and keeping friends: Temporal professed sixteen (55.17%), Novices fifteen (51.72%). "Tends to be needy": Temporal professed twenty (68.97%), Novices twenty-two (75.86%), and Postulants twenty-four (82.76%). "Recognition seeking": Temporal professed twenty-one (72.41%), Novices twenty (68.97%), Postulants sixteen (55.17%). "Fear of being judged": Temporal professed, nineteen (65.52%), and Novices seventeen (58.62%). "Gets sad/depressed easily and often": Temporal professed seventeen (58.62%), Novices nineteen (62.52%), and Postulants eleven (37.93%). "Anxious": Temporal professed twenty-one (72.41%), Novices and Postulants thirteen (44.83%) each. "Trust issues": Temporal professed twenty-one (72.41%), Novices sixteen (55.17%). "Feelings of abandonment": Temporal professed and Postulants ten (34.48%) each. "Lack of confidence" was peculiar to the temporal professed. Furthermore, some behaviors, though ticked, were not ticked proportionally.

Examples of such behaviors are "tend to be overly defensive," "feelings of being ridiculed," "feelings of loneliness," "fear of being judged," "feelings of worthlessness," "paranoid," "indecisive," "lacking coping skills," "crisis preoccupied," "emotionally inflexible," "tend to be very aggressive," "gives up too easily," "difficulty envisioning a future (self)," "routinely violates confidentiality," "not interested in what others feel," "inappropriate responses or behavior," "lacks enterprising spirit," "gets sad/depressed easily and often," "lacking purpose," "antisocial," "usually quiet and withdrawn," "too passive," "restless," "unhappy with choices made," "lacks leadership skills," "uncomfortable with oneself," "problem understanding," and "does not believe in oneself." "Tends to be overly defensive": Congregation five (17.24%), Final professed eleven (37.93%), Temporal professed ten (34.48%), Novices six (20.69%), Postulants twelve (41.38%), Own behavior ten (43.48%). "Feelings of being ridiculed": Congregation five (17.24%), Final professed seven (24.14%), Temporal professed three (10.34%), Novices twelve (41.38%),

Postulants eleven (37.93%), and Own eleven (37.93%). "Feelings of loneliness": Congregation eight (27.59%), Final professed two (6.90%), Temporal professed eleven (41.38%), Novices, thirteen (44.83%), Postulants nineteen (65.52%), and Own behavior seven (24.14%). "Feelings of being judged": Congregation one (3.43%), Final professed two (6.90%), Temporal professed nineteen (65.52%), Novices seventeen (58.62%), Postulants eight (27.59%) and Own behavior seven (24.14%). "Feelings of worthlessness": Congregation five (17.24%), Final professed eight (27.58%), Temporal professed fourteen (48.28%), Novices ten (34.48%), Postulants nine (31.03%), Own behavior six (20.69%). "Paranoid": Congregation six (20.69%), Final professed twelve (41.38%), Temporal professed nine (31.03%), Novices (not rated), Postulants ten (34.48%), and Own behavior five (17.24%). "Indecisive": Congregation seven (24.14%), Final professed four (13.79%), Temporal professed seven (24.14%), Novices nine (31.14%), Postulants eighteen (62.07%), and Own behavior two (6.90%). "Lacking coping skills": Congregation twelve (41.38%), Final professed seven (24.14%), Temporal professed seven (24.14%), Novices twelve (41.38%), Postulants twelve (41.38%), and Own behavior nine (31.03%). "Crisis preoccupied": Congregation six (20.69%), Final professed six (20.69%), Temporal professed five (17.24%), Novices (not rated), Postulants twelve (41.38%), and Own behavior two (6.90%). "Emotionally inflexible": Congregation three (10.34%), Final professed eight (27.59%), Temporal professed ten

(34.48%), Novices five (17.24%), Postulants twelve (41.38%), Own behavior ten (34.48%). "Tends to be verya ggressive": Congregation five (17.24%), Final professed six (30.68%), Temporal professed sixteen (55.17%), Novices ten (34.48%), Postulants fifteen (51.72%), Own behavior five (17.24%). "Gives up easily": Congregation five (17.24%), Final professed two (6.90%), Temporal professed five (17.24%), Novices (not rated), Postulants eight (27.59%), Own behavior six (30.68%). "Difficulty envisioning a future (self)": Congregation three (10.34%), Final professed four (13.79%), Temporal professed nine (31.03%), Novices seven (24.14%), Postulants eleven (37.93%), Own behavior two (6.90%). "Routinely violates confidentiality": Congregation five (17.24%), Final professed three (10.34%), Temporal professed twelve (41.38%), Novices seven (24.14%), Postulants twelve (41.38%), Own behavior six (20.69%). "Not interested in what others feel": Congregation six (20.69%), Final professed seven (24.14%), Temporal professed seven (24.14%), Novices six (20.69%), Postulants seven (24.14%), Own behavior twelve (41.38). "Inappropriate response or behavior": Congregation six (20.69%), Final professed seven (24.14%), Temporal professed two (6.90%), Novices seven (24.14%), Postulants four (48.28%), Own behavior eight (27.59%). "Lacks enterprising spirit": Congregation five (17.24%), Final professed (not rated), Temporal professed four (48.28%), Novices three (10.34%), Postulants seven (24.14%), and Own behavior three (10.34%). "Gets sad/ depressed easily and often": Congregation four (48.28%), Final professed one (3.45%), Temporal professed seventeen (58.62%), Novices nineteen (65.52%), Postulants eleven (37.93%), Own behavior eight (27.59%). "Lacking purpose": Congregation five (17.24%), Final professed three (10.34%), Temporal professed nine (31.03%), Novices nine (31.03%, Postulants six (20.69%), Own behavior five (17.24%). "Antisocial": Congregation two (6.90%), Final professed eight (27.59%), Temporal professed eight (27.59%), Novices five (17.24%), Postulants three (10.34%), Own behavior eight (27.59%). "Usually quiet and withdrawn": Congregation six (20.69%), Final professed eight (27.59%), Temporal professed three (10.34%), Novices two (6.90%), Postulants four (48.28%), Own behavior nine (31.03%). "Too passive": Congregation seven (24.14%), Final professed six (20.69%), Temporal professed six (20.69%), Novices (not rated), Postulants (not rated), Own behavior four (48.28%). "Restless": Congregation six (20.69%), Final professed four (48.28%), Temporal professed six (20.69%), Novices three (10.34%), Postulants four (48.28%), Own behavior three (10.34%). "Unhappy with choices made": Congregation four (48.28%), Final professed two (6.90%), Temporal professed ten (34.48%), Novices six (20.69%), Postulants twelve (41.38%), Own behavior three (10.34%). "Lacks leadershipskills": Congregation seven (24.14%), Final professed three (10.34%), Temporal professed six (20.69%), Novices fourteen (48.28%), Postulants fourteen (48.28%), and Own behavior three (10.34%). "Uncomfortable with oneself": Congregation (not rated), Final professed four (48.28%), Temporal professed three (10.34%), Novices six (20.69%), Postulants ten (34.48%), Own behavior six (20.69%). "Problems not understanding": Congregation eleven (37.93%), Final professed five (17.24%), Temporal professed seven (24.14%), Novices thirteen (44.83%), Postulants nine (31.03%), Own behavior five (17.24%). "Does not believe in oneself": Congregation twelve (41.38%), Final professed four (13.79%), Temporal professed seven (24.14%), Novices eleven (37.93%), Postulants thirteen (44.83%), Own behavior six (20.69%).

Respondents' own behaviors also received a high number of responses. The highest number of respondents ticked "unable to handle crises," followed by "difficulty making and keeping friends" and "recognition seeking." Next are "emotionally distant," "trust issues," "crisis preoccupied," "inability to control one's emotions," "fear of being involved," and "not interested in what others feel," all with twelve (41.38%). The next most common behaviors are "tends to be needy," "self-blaming," "feelings of being ridiculed," "suffers from mood swings, with eleven (37.93%) each. Next are "tends to be overly defensive," "untrusting," "discipline or retaliating by shaming," and "emotionally inflexible," all with ten (34.48%) each. The next were "tends to get into other people's stuff" and "lacking coping skills," with nine (31.03%). The next most common behaviors are "anxious," "too sensitive," "inappropriate responses or behavior," "gets sad/depressed easily and often," and "antisocial," with eight (27.59%) each. Some behaviors were not selected by many respondents, but it is worth noting that they are present, such as "feelings of loneliness," "fear of being judged," "problem adapting to various feelings," and "controlling." The next most common behaviors are "tends to be angry most of the time," "low self-esteem," "feelings of worthlessness," "does not believe in oneself," "routinely violated confidentiality," "gives up too easily," "self-centeredness," and "uncomfortable with oneself," all with six (20.69%) each. Other behaviors were selected by very few respondents: "problem understanding," "paranoid," "tends to be very aggressive," and "lacking purpose." The next selected behaviors are "restless," "suffers from feelings of abandonment," and "too passive," with four (13.79%) each. Next are "disinterested in being a good role model," "lacks leadership skills," "unhappy with choices made," "difficulty being alone," and "lacks enterprising spirit," with three (10.34%) each. The behaviors that were selected least are "difficulty envisioning a future self," "crisis preoccupied," and "indecisive," with two responses (6.90%) each.

The researcher observed a low number of responses among the congregations in certain behaviors. The behaviors "paranoid," "crisis preoccupied," "not interested in what others feel," "inappropriate responses or behavior," "usually quiet and withdrawn," and "restless" were all selected six times (20.69%) each. The next group of behaviors includes "tends to be overly defensive," "feelings of being ridiculed," "feelings of worthlessness," "routinely violates confidentiality," "tends to be very aggressive," and "gives up easily," all of which were ticked five times (17.24%). The behaviors "lacking purpose" and "unhappy with choices made" were each chosen four times (48.28%), while "emotionally inflexible" and "difficulty envisioning a future self" each got three (10.34%) ticks. The behaviors selected the least number of times are "antisocial," "disinterested in being a good role model," and "suffers from feelings of abandonment," with two selections (6.9%) each, and "difficulty being alone" and "fear of being judged," each with one selection (3.45%).

Similarly, the data also revealed that some behaviors were prevalent to final professed sisters: "fear of being involved," "tends to get into other people's stuff," "trust issues," "talks too much and listens too little," "paranoid," "unable to handle crises," "inability to control one's emotions," "controlling," and "too sensitive." The behavior selected most often was "fear of being involved," at twenty-seven (93.10%), and the next was "talks too much and listens too little," with fifteen (51.72%). The next most prevalent behaviors were "trust issues" and "tends to get into other people's stuff," each with thirteen (44.83%) each. After these, "paranoid" and "unable to handle crises" were each selected twelve times (41.38%) each. With eleven selections (37.93%), the "inability to control one's emotions" followed. Next were "too sensitive" and "controlling," with ten (34.48%) each. "Suffers from mood swings" was selected nine times (31.03%), and five behaviors were equally prevalent, with eight selections "indecisive." They each were selected four (13.79%) times. Some of the least prevalent behaviors were "lacks leadership skills," "difficulty being alone," "lacking purpose," and "problem adapting to various feelings," with three (10.34%) each, and "suffers from feelings of abandonment," "unhappy with choices made," "gives up easily," "fear of being judged," and "feelings of loneliness" each elicited two (6.90%) responses. Last was "gets sad/depressed easily and often," with one (3.45%) response. It is clear that not only people in formation exhibit these behaviors; people in final vows (professed) do as well, even though some behaviors were not prevalent. Some categories of respondents did not select some behaviors at all. "Tends to get into other people's stuff" and "disinterested in being a good role model" were not selected by postulants, while "paranoid," "crisis preoccupied," "gives up easily," "too passive," and "disinterested in being a good role model" were not chosen at all by novices. Final professed did not select "lacks an enterprising spirit" or "disinterested in being a good role model." Similarly, congregations did not select "uncomfortable with oneself."

It is worth noting that much is at stake for those in formation: temporal professed, novices, and postulants or candidates. They are frequently sent home randomly, so there is usually fear and anxiety among them since they are not sure of their fates. They will try to put on false selves in other to become finally professed, where they are less likely to be expelled or let go. If an individual who is finally professed needs to go home or be expelled, she needs to be dispensed from her vows by the Holy See (Rome) if her congregation has a pontifical status. But if it is a diocesan congregation, what is stated in the constitution holds. It is always easier to be expelled.

We now move to the group of respondents who grew up with their fathers. Out of the 178 responses received, 149 (83.71%) indicated that they had grown up with fathers. This group answered the first question regarding what they experienced with their fathers while growing up in their home environments.

<u>TABLE 3. Experiences with fathers</u>

|  | # | % |
| --- | --- | --- |
| My father supported and encouraged me to be a leader. | 142 | 95.30 |
| My father was a positive role model for me. | 140 | 93.96 |
| My father was affectionate and played with me. | 113 | 75.84 |
| My father spent time listening to me and having conversation with me. | 115 | 77.18 |
| My father would show up at my school and community activities and performances. | 98 | 65.77 |

| | | |
|---|---|---|
| My father encouraged me to do good at whatever I was doing. | 121 | 81.21 |
| My father publicly rebuked or shamed me when I made mistakes. | 42 | 28.19 |
| My father punished me when I made mistakes. | 103 | 69.13 |
| My father encouraged me to do better when I made mistakes or fell short. | 112 | 75.17 |
| My father prevented or discouraged me from doing or pursuing things I like. | 18 | 12.08 |
| My father was present in the home but did not interact positively with me. | 11 | 7.38 |
| My father drove fear into me. | 21 | 14.09 |
| My father tried to control what I did and how I did it. | 71 | 47.65 |
| My father made me feel inadequate or not good enough. | - | - |
| My father physically abused me. | 2 | 1.34 |

Table 3 indicates that the majority of respondents ticked the favorable statements. "My father supported and encouraged me to be a leader" elicited the most responses, with 142 (93.3%), followed by "My father was a positive role model in my life," at 140 (93.96%). The next most-selected statement was "My father spent time listening to me and having conversation with me," with 115 (77.18%) respondents choosing it. After that was "My father was affectionate and playful with me," with 113 (75.84%). Similarly, 121 (81.21%) respondents ticked the positive statement, "My father encouraged me to do good at whatever I was doing, and "My father encouraged me to do better when I made mistakes or fell short" elicited 112 (75.17%) responses. Also, among the positive statements, 98 (65.77%) respondents experienced their fathers' showing up at their school and community activities and performances, which was the least selected.

Among the not-so-positive experiences that respondents who grew up with their fathers had, "My father punished me when I made mistakes" was the most selected, with 103 (69.13%) respondents indicating they had this experience. This means that even though the respondents said they had positive influences, they also had negative ones, which brings us to the fact that a child can be confused by the caregivers' inconsistent positivity. This leads to doubt in the growing child. The next most-selected statement, with 71 (47.65%), was "My father tried to control what I did and how I did it," followed by "My father publicly rebuked or shamed me when I made mistakes," with 42 (28.19%). "My father drove fear into me" was selected by 21 (14.09%) respondents, and "My father prevented or discouraged me from doing or pursuing things I liked" was chosen by 18 (12.08%). It is significant that even though "My father was present in the home but did not interact positively" received few selections, at 11 (7.38%), it gives us a glimpse of what happens in the homes of unavailable or emotionally absent caregivers.

One of the least rated, with 6 (4.03%) selections, was "My father did not show me that he loved me," and 2 (1.34%) ticked "My father physically abused me." Last, "My father made me feel inadequate or not good enough" was not selected by any respondents.

Now we consider the behaviors that those who grew up with their fathers have observed in their congregations-in others and in themselves.

TABLE 4. Behaviors and responses of those who grew up with fathers

| | Congregation | | Final professed | | Temporal professed | | Novices | | Postulants | | My own | |
|---|---|---|---|---|---|---|---|---|---|---|---|---|
| | # | % | # | % | # | % | # | % | # | % | # | % |
| Untrusting | 82 | 55.00 | 75 | 50.00 | 49 | 32.89 | 35 | 23.49 | 23 | 15.44 | 31 | 20.81 |
| Difficulty making and keeping friends | 46 | 30.87 | 31 | 20.81 | 26 | 17.45 | 32 | 21.48 | 27 | 18.12 | 21 | 14.09 |
| Tends to be angry most of the time | 52 | 34.90 | 51 | 34.23 | 29 | 19.46 | 14 | 9.40 | 7 | 4.70 | 25 | 16.78 |
| Tends to be needy | 77 | 51.68 | 54 | 36.24 | 40 | 26.85 | 33 | 22.15 | 32 | 21.48 | 29 | 19.46 |
| Tends to be overly defensive | 60 | 40.27 | 67 | 44.97 | 35 | 23.49 | 26 | 17.45 | 15 | 10.07 | 27 | 18.42 |
| Tends to be very aggressive | 50 | 33.56 | 58 | 38.93 | 34 | 22.82 | 24 | 16.11 | 11 | 7.38 | 26 | 17.45 |
| Recognition seeking | 54 | 38.26 | 53 | 35.57 | 56 | 37.58 | 43 | 28.86 | 26 | 17.45 | 29 | 19.46 |
| Anxious | 64 | 42.95 | 59 | 39.60 | 67 | 44.97 | 74 | 49.66 | 52 | 34.90 | 66 | 44.30 |
| Low self esteem | 42 | 28.19 | 35 | 30.20 | 42 | 28.19 | 29 | 19.46 | 45 | 30.20 | 31 | 20.81 |
| Feelings of being ridiculed | 41 | 27.52 | 33 | 22.15 | 32 | 21.48 | 29 | 19.46 | 29 | 19.46 | 18 | 12.08 |
| Emotionally distant or unavailable | 48 | 32.21 | 41 | 27.52 | 34 | 22.82 | 19 | 12.75 | 13 | 8.72 | 27 | 18.12 |
| Tends to get into other people's stuff | 76 | 51.01 | 64 | 42.95 | 42 | 28.19 | 18 | 12.08 | 9 | 6.40 | 27 | 18.12 |
| Discipline or retaliating by shaming | 56 | 37.58 | 39 | 26.17 | 24 | 16.11 | 24 | 16.11 | 13 | 8.72 | 15 | 10.07 |
| Feelings of loneliness | 34 | 22.82 | 29 | 19.46 | 18 | 12.08 | 21 | 14.09 | 24 | 16.11 | 17 | 11.41 |
| Fear of being judged | 27 | 18.12 | 46 | 30.87 | 42 | 28.19 | 42 | 28.19 | 37 | 24.83 | 36 | 24.16 |
| Feelings of worthlessness | 8 | 5.37 | 24 | 16.11 | 14 | 9.40 | 5 | 3.36 | 9 | 6.04 | 5 | 3.36 |
| Paranoid | 45 | 30.20 | 52 | 34.90 | 19 | 12.75 | 12 | 5.05 | 11 | 7.58 | 29 | 19.46 |
| Indecisive | 35 | 23.49 | 36 | 24.16 | 28 | 18.79 | 19 | 12.75 | 41 | 27.52 | 23 | 15.44 |
| Lacking coping skills | 31 | 20.81 | 36 | 24.16 | 33 | 22.15 | 36 | 24.16 | 32 | 21.48 | 28 | 18.79 |
| Suffers from mood swings | 39 | 26.17 | 35 | 23.49 | 24 | 16.11 | 29 | 19.46 | 16 | 10.74 | 27 | 18.12 |
| Trust issues | 82 | 55.03 | 69 | 46.31 | 61 | 40.94 | 38 | 25.50 | 33 | 22.15 | 55 | 36.91 |
| Crisis preoccupied | 49 | 32.89 | 22 | 14.71 | 32 | 21.48 | 12 | 8.05 | 14 | 9.40 | 20 | 13.42 |
| Unable to handle crises | 55 | 36.91 | 33 | 22.15 | 57 | 38.26 | 43 | 28.86 | 42 | 28.19 | 34 | 22.82 |
| Fear of getting involved | 57 | 38.26 | 55 | 36.91 | 45 | 30.20 | 69 | 45.64 | 55 | 36.91 | 49 | 32.89 |
| Fear of rejection | 50 | 33.56 | 26 | 17.45 | 46 | 30.87 | 60 | 40.27 | 44 | 29.53 | 34 | 22.82 |
| Does not believe in oneself | 37 | 24.83 | 33 | 22.15 | 40 | 26.85 | 26 | 17.45 | 32 | 21.48 | 24 | 16.11 |
| Problems understanding | 49 | 32.89 | 57 | 38.26 | 37 | 24.85 | 18 | 12.08 | 23 | 15.44 | 39 | 26.17 |
| Lacking self confidence | 40 | 26.85 | 37 | 24.83 | 49 | 32.89 | 44 | 29.53 | 43 | 28.56 | 39 | 26.17 |
| Emotionally inflexible | 39 | 26.17 | 22 | 14.77 | 36 | 24.16 | 21 | 14.09 | 19 | 12.75 | 12 | 8.05 |
| Routinely violates confidentiality | 43 | 28.86 | 36 | 24.16 | 25 | 16.78 | 14 | 9.40 | 21 | 14.09 | 10 | 6.71 |
| Difficulty envisioning a future (self) | 17 | 11.41 | 16 | 10.74 | 19 | 12.75 | 13 | 8.72 | 16 | 10.74 | 11 | 7.38 |
| Gives up easily | 42 | 28.19 | 46 | 30.87 | 39 | 26.17 | 37 | 24.83 | 44 | 29.53 | 55 | 36.91 |
| Too sensitive | 72 | 48.32 | 60 | 40.27 | 50 | 33.56 | 29 | 19.46 | 26 | 17.45 | 52 | 34.90 |
| Not interested in what others feel | 60 | 40.27 | 58 | 38.90 | 25 | 16.78 | 6 | 4.03 | 15 | 10.07 | 28 | 18.79 |
| Likes to fix other people's problems | 71 | 47.65 | 60 | 40.27 | 29 | 19.46 | 8 | 5.37 | 17 | 11.41 | 39 | 26.17 |
| Talks too much and listens too little | 80 | 53.69 | 73 | 48.99 | 34 | 22.82 | 12 | 8.05 | 18 | 12.08 | 27 | 18.12 |
| Inappropriate responses or behavior | 36 | 24.16 | 40 | 26.85 | 21 | 14.08 | 11 | 7.38 | 14 | 9.40 | 14 | 9.40 |

Table 4 describes the behaviors that were observed by the sisters in their various congregations who grew up with their fathers in the home. The behaviors they noticed are very different from those who did not grow up with their fathers. For these respondents, behaviors that were most prevalent as per their observations of their congregations was "controlling," "untrusting," and "trust issues." After those, the next most-prevalent behaviors were "talks too much and listens too little" and "tends to be needy." Agreement was also high on the behavior of "tends to get into other people's stuff." "Too sensitive" was ticked often, as were "likes to fix other people's problems" and "tends to be overly defensive." "Discipline by retaliating or shaming" came in next, followed by "lack of leadership skills" as the least prevalent.

"Unable to handle crises" received numerous responses, and "tends to be very aggressive" was selected by a little more than a third of respondents in congregations and in final professed. Next came "lack of leadership skills" and "self-centeredness." One group of behaviors elicited almost even responses: "lacking coping skills," "fear of getting involved," "gives up easily," "lack of self-confidence," and "low self-esteem." It is interesting to note that, of "recognition seeking" and "anxious," the groups that most noticed these behaviors were temporal professed and novices because they must always be ready to exit and are most often unsure of themselves. As a result, these individuals frequently attach themselves to those in authority so they will be favored. The data also indicated that numerous respondents saw many of these behaviors in themselves. The most prevalent in this group was "anxious" with sixty-six (44.38%) selections, followed by "trust issues" and "gives up easily," at fifty-five (36.91%) each. These were followed by "too sensitive," fifty- two (34.90%); "fear of getting involved," forty-nine (32.89%); and "inability to control one's emotions," forty-two (28.19%). The next most common were "difficulty understanding," "likes to fix other people's problems," and "lack of self-confidence," each selected by thirty-nine (26.17%) respondents. Following were "fear of being judged," thirty- six (24.16%); "unable to handle crises" and "fear of rejection," thirty-four (22.82%) each; "lacks leadership skills," thirty-two (21.48%); and "untrusting," thirty-one (20.81%). Some own behaviors were not selected by many respondents, like "controlling," "paranoid," "recognition seeking," and "tends to be needy," each with twenty-nine (19.465); "lacking coping skills," "not interested in what others feel," and "problems adapting to various feelings," with twenty-eight (18.79%) each. Other nonprevalent behaviors were "emotionally distant or unavailable," "tends to get into other people's stuff," "tends to be overly defensive," "suffers from mood swings," and "talks too much and listens too little," each with twenty-seven (18.42%) selections. "Tends to be very aggressive," with twenty-six (17.45%); "suffers from feelings of abandonment" and "tends to be angry most of the time," with twenty-five (16.78%) each; "does not believe in oneself," with twenty- four (16.11%); "gets sad/depressed easily and often" and "indecisive," with twenty-three (15.44%) each; "usually quiet and withdrawn," with twenty-two (14.77%); "difficulty keeping and making friends," with twenty-one (14.09%); and "self-centeredness" and "crisis occupied," each with twenty (13.42%). Some of the least commonly noticed behaviors were "feelings of being ridiculed," eighteen (12.08%); "feelings of loneliness," seventeen (11.41%); "too passive," sixteen (10.74%); "discipline by retaliating or shaming," fifteen (10.07%); "inappropriate responses or behavior," fourteen (9.40%); "emotionally inflexible" and "lacking purpose," twelve (8.05%) each; "difficulty envisioning a future (self)," eleven (7.38%); and "routinely violates confidentiality," "restless," and "difficulty being alone," ten

(6.71%) each. Even less common were "unhappy with choices made," eight (5.37%); "lacks the enterprising spirit" and "antisocial," six (4.03%) each; "feelings of worthlessness," five (3.36%); and "disinterested in being a good role model" and "uncomfortable with oneself," four (2.68%).

It is interesting to note the most prevalent behaviors noticed by those in congregations. At the top of that list are "controlling," eighty- eight (59.06%); "trust issues" and "untrusting," eighty-two (55.03%) each; "talks too much and listens too little," eighty (53.69%); "tends to be needy," seventy-seven (51.68%); "tends to get into other people's stuff," seventy-six (51.01%); "too sensitive," seventy-two (48.32%); and "likes to fix other people's problems," seventy-one (47.65%). The next most commonly noticed behaviors are "anxious," sixty-four (42.95%); "self-centeredness," sixty-two (41.64%); "not interested in what others feel" and "tends to be overly defensive," sixty (40.27%) each. The next ones are "lacks leadership skills," fifty- nine (39.60%); "fear of getting involved," fifty-seven (38.26%); "discipline or retaliating by shaming," fifty-six (37.58%); "unable to handle crises," fifty-five (36.91%); "recognition seeking," fifty-four (38.26%); "tends to be angry most of the time," fifty-two (34.90%); and "tends to be aggressive" and "fear of rejection," fifty (33.56%) each.

Non-prevalent behaviors among the congregations were "difficulty making and keeping friends," forty-six (30.87%); "emotionally distant or unavailable," forty- eight (32.21%); "paranoid," forty-five (30.20%); "crisis preoccupied," forty-nine (32.89%); "problems understanding," forty- nine (32.89%); "routinely violates confidentiality," forty-three (28.86%); and "low self-esteem" and "gives up easily rated," forty-two (28.19%) each. Other behaviors that were not commonly noticed were "emotionally inflexible" and "suffers from mood swings," thirty-nine (26.17%) each; "suffers from feelings of abandonment," thirty-eight (25.50%); "does not believe in oneself," thirty-seven (24.83%); "inappropriate responses or behavior," "problem adapting to various feelings," and "lacks an enterprising spirit," thirty-six (24.16%) each; "indecisive," thirty-five (23.49%); "too passive" and "feelings of loneliness," thirty-four (22.82%) each; "lacking coping skills," "difficulty being alone," and "lacking purpose," thirty-one (20.81%) each; "anti-social," thirty (20.13%); "fear of being judged," twenty-seven (18.12%); "disinterested in being a good role model" and "unhappy with choices made," twenty-five (16.78%) each; and "uncomfortable with oneself," twenty-one (14.09). The least prevalent behaviors were "restless," nineteen (12.75%); "difficulty envisioning a future (self)," seventeen (11.41%); and "feelings of worthlessness," eight (5.37%).

Other behaviors, although not highly prevalent, were still significant among the final professed sisters, showing that these behaviors exist in these congregations. Final professed sisters have much power in their various congregations. In fact, it is from this group that leaders of each congregation are chosen or voted for. Most often, these behaviors create problems for those in formation, and their predictions hold. The behaviors these sisters noted are "low self-esteem," "feelings of being ridiculed," "emotionally distant or unavailable," "discipline by retaliating or shaming," "feelings of loneliness," "fear of being judged," "indecisive," "lacking coping skills," "suffers from mood swings," "unable to handle crises," "does not believe in oneself," "lacking self-confidence," "gives up easily," "inappropriate responses or behaviors," "lacking purpose," "antisocial," "usually quiet and withdrawn," "lacks leadership skills," "feelings of loneliness," "too passive," "lacks the enterprising spirit," "gets sad/depressed often and easily," and "inability to control one's emotions."

"Fear of being judged" and "gives up easily" were noted by forty-six respondents (30.87%) each. "Lacks leadership skills" and "emotionally distant or unavailable" followed closely with forty-one (27.52%). Following those were "inappropriate responses or behavior," forty (26.85%); "routinely violates confidentiality" and "discipline by shaming or retaliating," thirty-nine (26.17%) each, "lacking self-confidence" and "inability to control one's emotions," thirty-seven (24.83%) each; "indecisive," "routinely violates confidentiality," and "lacking coping skills," thirty-six (24.16%) each; "low self- esteem," "suffers from mood swings," and "usually quiet and withdrawn," thirty-five (23.49%) each; "feelings of being ridiculed," "unable to handle crises," and "does not believe in oneself," thirty-three (22.15%) each; "lacking purpose," "antisocial," and "difficulty making and keeping friends," thirty-one (20.81%) each; "feelings of loneliness," twenty-nine (19.46%); "lacks the enterprising spirit," "gets sad/depressed easily and often," and "too passive," twenty- eight (18.79%).

**Case Study**

This is a case study of an actual encounter between a patient and the researcher, showing how an emotionally absent father and mother can affect a growing child. The patient presented herself at the clinic for her initial intake as a single, moderately employed, heterosexual woman of mixed race residing in her own apartment. She is a Christian but does not practice. She reported that she has been depressed and anxious all her life. She added that her parents did not want her as early as she was conceived. She reported that, at an early age, she was abandoned by her father. Owing to this, she lacks self-confidence and has low self-esteem issues. This abandonment has affected her relationships with others, men included. The patient said in our meeting that her mother's first sexual experience resulted in pregnancy, and she was not prepared for it.

The patient's relatives prevented the patient's mother from aborting the growing fetus, even though she had tried to. An older lady in the family cared for the patient for the first six years of her life. When she met her mother at the age of six upon the death of the caregiver, her mother treated her like a second-class citizen, always reminding her how she has ruined her life. She said that getting pregnant resulted in lost opportunities for good things to come into her life. The patient's mother never loved her. The mother had won the first round of a beauty pageant and was waiting for the second round when she got pregnant. In the mother's eyes, the pregnancy became the patient's fault. The patient felt she was a stranger in the home. There was no connection. She always felt she had a hole in her heart. She referred to her mother as abusive, harsh, critical, vicious, angry, unhappy, and unloving. The patient's mother was not able to give her the protection, nurturing, and care she needed, nor could she give her "the deepest thing in human nature-togetherness" (Guntrip 1995, 269). In the twenty-fifth session, she cried, "Why can't anyone love me?" From very early in her life, the mother had not been a good- enough mother to her. In school, she was bullied for her brown skin and referred to as fat, ugly, and dumb. She said, "I did not do well in school. No one helped me to do my homework. My school life was awful and horrible. My mother was not there when I cried and needed help." She had to run away from home and began to abuse alcohol, marijuana, cigars, and then cocaine. She had developed this way of life to safeguard her fragile self. The patient's mother had not achieved any connection with her as a fetus growing in the womb, an infant, or a baby. The mother's lack of a sense of self thwarted her ability to be attuned to her daughter's developmental needs. When a mother becomes the abuser, it is shocking for the child. "Suddenly the hand that should be caressing curls into a fist. Or it reaches for a belt, a coat hanger, a wooden spoon. The woman whose love should be a given looks at you, or through you, nothing, in her gaze but rage and she hits.... Common kitchen objects turn into weapons.... Mother becomes monster, and a world that need be safe shatters" (Forward 2014, 119). This was the horrifying case of the patient in the early years as a girl.

The patient's early and adolescent years were characterized by chronic and traumatic deprivation. The researcher worked with her in the initial phase of the treatment to establish a strong therapeutic alliance and provide ego-supportive therapy. In working with her, the researcher became the good- enough mother and, as such, listened to the painful, unhappy, and damaged aspects of her life—both the spoken and the unspoken aspects. The researcher shared in her experience from the intersubjectivity stance. Intersubjectivity is the ability to share in another person's lived experience.

Daniel Stein defines *intersubjectivity* as "the capacity to share, know, understand, empathize with, feel, participate in, resonate with, and enter into the lived subjective experience of another" (1998, 78). Imagine the terror of a little girl of six years being subjected to inhuman treatment of pain and abuse by her own mother and being sexually violated by an older person without knowing whom to talk to because she dreads her mother's abuse. The researcher became a container and a holding environment for her (Winnicott), watching the patient grow to understand herself and choose to change her relationship dynamics.

A lot of transferences go on in religious communities without being noticed. If an analyst is available to provide interpretations of some of the behaviors, sisters in those communities will begin to understand the dynamics of their relationships, thus minimizing chaos. The following is an example of a transference experienced by the researcher in her work with a patient. This interaction (intersubjectivity) helped the patient in her recovery.

The patient was an adolescent who was single and part-time employed. She was slender, attractive, average in height, and relatively well groomed. She presented as tense and nervous and at the same time smiled inappropriately during sessions. She was born in a habitat. She did not finish high school. In both primary and high school, she was made fun of. She was ridiculed and called fat, ugly, and colored. She tried to finish her education but could not.

Nothing she tried to do worked. She was not accepted by her family of origin and so had to take care of herself.

Psychoanalytically, the patient has abandonment issues. She had insecure and anxious attachment and no secure base. Her parents were unable to present her with consistent, stable, adequate, and nurturing care, and as such she was unable to develop basic trust that people are trustworthy and dependable. She did not have the capacity to trust herself and others and, as a result, was unable to develop a sense of confidence. The patient could no longer tolerate the effects of her rejection, her intense deprivation, or her sense of unworthiness and inadequacy. She could no longer live with her anger and fear that she might hurt herself and others. She could not manage her rage that madc hcr depressed, and so she had to come for therapy.

**Experience of a Transference and Therapist's Interpretation in Session**

In one of the therapy sessions, an emergency came up, so the therapist let the patient know and asked her permission for a few minutes before finishing the session with her.

**Therapist:** Please, there is an emergency with the patient after you, and I have been called to attend to him until he is all right. I am asking permission to leave the session, but I will give you your full forty-five minutes.

**J. A.:** Sure.

(The therapist attended to the emergency and returned ten minutes later to continue with J. A.'s session. She blurted out in anger.)

**J. A.:** I am always taken advantage of. I am always taken for granted. I know I do not matter. No one seems to notice me.

**Therapist:** Do you feel not noticed and taken for granted?

**J. A:** I think the person outside the room is more important than me.

**Therapist:** Because you are as important as the person outside, I did not leave without letting you know it was an emergency, and I promised to give you the time I will use. The emergency did not mean I did not care about you. It felt to you that I had abandoned you to attend to another person.

The therapist and J. A. talked about J. A.'s feelings of not being accepted and wanted in the session, and the therapist explained that attending to an emergency did not mean she did not care about her.

J. A. narrated a story of how, as a child in school, she had presented her work to her teacher. As the teacher reviewed the work, the teacher was called outside and never got back to J. A. and her work. She said she felt unimportant, unnoticed, and ignored as all the students rushed out of the class, leaving her and her work alone in the class. The therapist made her understand that her past experiences were coming up in the present. This interpretation helped J. A. understand more about herself and how she related to situations.

131

*Chapter 5*

## Summary of the Work and Discussion

### Discussion and Summary of the Work

The following findings correspond to the proposed research hypotheses.

### *Hypothesis Number 1*

Children raised in unstable homes without proper care and nurturing love tend to suffer chronic emotional insufficiency in their adult lives even when they choose to live a religious life.

An unstable home for a child is a home that is physically, emotionally, and socially unsafe for the child, a home where children are exposed to a threatening environment, where anger is expressed, for example, by throwing things or hitting others. It is a home where fear, parental neglect, abuse, rejection, and a lack of consistently adequate or good-enough love and care is the order of the day. An unstable home environment affects children's emotional development, placing their development at risk. There is always an emotional deficit (Erikson 1994; Winnicott 2005). An unstable home has a lack of proper care and nurturing love. There is a lack of trust, and the home is full of mistrust (lack of Erikson's first stage of psychosocial development). A lack of proper care and nurturing love makes for a home where children feel unloved and uncared for emotionally, which results in chronic emotional insufficiency-leaving children to crave love and attention. They will develop mistrust (Erikson's psychosocial theory; Winnicott's lack of capacity to believe). "Not having received much support as children leaves the undermothered with a less confident sense of self and less inner support because there wasn't a good-enough mother to internalize" (Cori 2010, 111).

This is the experience of another patient:

*I was six years old, and it was Thanksgiving. We were all at a table, with my family and my mother's boyfriend. There was a guest who had joined us. I did not know who my father was or where he was. I was a "lefty," meaning I use my left hand in doing things. All of a sudden the guest yelled at me and said, "You are a child of the devil because you use your left hand to eat, and God will rain down thunder and lightning on you. You are an evil child, and you must be treated like one." I answered him, "Sir, I am a child of God." He got up and slapped me. My mother did not defend me. All through my life I had believed I was evil. I had lived a very destructive life as a mother myself until I sought help a few years ago. I had always felt unloved and unwanted. I was just like my mother.*

Forward explains, "Daughters of controlling mothers almost universally promise themselves one thing... I will never turn into my mother.... As adults, they often shock themselves by acting very much the way their mothers did toward them" (2014, 78). This patient had no sense of value, felt she did not matter, and believed that something was wrong with her.

All of this was due to the parent's inability to manage the home environment. According to Cori, "A mother can profess to be very loving and involved with her child, and she can gain considerable recognition from the world for this, but the child will feel a hole in his soul when Mommy's love isn't genuine. It doesn't matter how many pronouncements mother makes.... If there isn't a sense of real contact and caring the child will not experience Mother as a source of nurturance" (2010, 31). Chapman and Campbell adds, "In raising children everything depends on the love relationship between the parent and the child. Nothing works well if a child's love needs are not met. Only the loved and cared for can do her best. You may love your child but unless she feels it-unless you speak the love language that communicates to her your love-she will not feel loved" (2005, 16). Bowlby has this to say: "For those who have children but fail to rear them to be healthy, happy, and self-reliant the penalties in anxiety, frustration, friction, and perhaps shame and guilt, may be severe" (1988, 1). He adds that "unsuccessful parenting is a key to the mental health of the next generation" (Bowlby 1988, 1). Anderson made this observation: "How can you tell when a child has no home? How can you tell when a child is done. How can you tell when a child is abused. How can you tell when a child has nothing to call her own?" (2008, 175).

Forward says, "Girls define their emerging womanhood by identifying and bonding with their moms. But when that vital process is distorted because their mothers are abusive, critical, smothering, depressed, neglectful, or distant-they're left to struggle alone to try to find a solid sense of themselves and their place in the world" (2014, 4).

The research supports the above hypothesis, as does the case study. The questionnaire showed some of the manifestations of adults who have chosen the religious life and who have chronic emotional insufficiency. We take into consideration both those who grew up with their fathers and those who did not. The chart shows that choosing to enter religious life does not erase the deficit an individual has acquired in her growing up, especially if the person is from a very inconsistent environment. Both Erikson and Winnicott made us aware that an individual needs to pass through the crises of the psychosocial stages successfully as well as achieve the six capacities. The findings correspond to the hypothesis.

**Hypothesis Number 2**

Unless an individual has a secure base while growing up with an intuitive and understanding caregiver, that individual is likely to face emotional turmoil as an adult.

A secure base is established in the way an infant attaches to her mother. It is the mother-infant attachment and the process through which it is achieved. The child feels loved and cared for by the primary caregiver. The child feels welcomed, understood, and wanted. "Attachment for the young child brings the feelings of 'I belong to you. And because I belong to you, I have a place'" (Cori 2010, 24). Secure base means reliability, consistency, and safety. An intuitive and understanding caregiver is one who can instinctively sense or recognize a child's needs.

When a mother is narcissistic; is herself insecure and self-doubting; has an insatiable need for approval, adoration, and praise; constantly needs to be the center of attention; and has a need to block her daughter's developing confidence and self-worth, she not only makes her daughter feel unloved but also makes her feel unimportant since her mother always pushes her aside while she fills the spotlight. The maternal preoccupation and good-enough mothering Winnicott talks about (Winnicott 1986), and its continuity, gives the child the secure base. The lack of it creates emotional turmoil. "Without this we are untethered, adrift well into our adult years" (Cori 2010, 24). She adds, "When mother does not celebrate our ordinary successes, we may feel invisible or that we have to accomplish extraordinary things (good or bad) to get her attentions" (Cori 2010, 35). Emotional turmoil or chaos is a feeling of not being supported, a feeling of confusion, agitation, and panic.

Greenberg and Mitchell affirms that "when there has been unavailable or arbitrary parenting there is a profound disturbance in relating" (1983, 156). This is the claim of one patient: "My mother is abusive, critical, vicious, angry, and unhappy and makes sure I am also not happy." Anderson asks us to consider, if a mother tells a child, "Ain't you glad I changed my mind 'bout the abortion when I was carrying you?" (2008, 37), how would the child feel all her life? Anderson spoke of her own mother thusly: "One of my mother's strengths was her ability to manipulate people and convince them to do whatever she wanted" (2008, 22). She added, "She used her looks to get whatever she wanted.... She used her position to get in and out of stuff.... She wanted me to be as miserable as she was" (2008, 22). Bradshaw says, "When a child's development is arrested, when feelings are repressed, especially the feelings of anger and hurt, a person grows up to be an adult with an angry, hurt child inside of him. This child will spontaneously contaminate the person's adult life" (1990, 7). "All your life you've ... been trapped in the belief that, you, not your mother, are flawed. This damaged self-image shaped your developing sense of yourself as a woman, which you carried into adulthood like a steamer trunk: And from that early collections of fears... about yourself, you continue to orchestrate many of the self-defeating behaviors of your life" (Forward 2014, 19).

Both Winnicott (2005) and Erikson (1980) talked about the good-enough mother and mothering, using different terms, and how it can give a child a secure base. For Erikson, a good enough mother is a mother who can meet the needs of her baby, that is, who makes sure the baby is held, fed, smiled at, rocked, and so forth. For Winnicott, when the good-enough mother meets the day-to-day needs of her infant, the true self gradually grows, whereas a lack of it creates a false self. To form emotional stability, according to Winnicott, a child needs to internalize a constant and positive image of the mother. This consistency confirms Winnicott's capacity to believe as well as the capacity to use others and be used (1986), which pave the way for this individual in adult life to be depended upon by others since the basis for dependability has been established in the child's life. One who experiences emotional turmoil or chaos has difficulty making decisions and constant anxiety. The individual loses control over her emotions and behaves impulsively. This means that Erikson's second psychosocial stage, shame and doubt versus autonomy, was not achieved. When parents overstep their control of the child's activities, the child may revert to insecurity and a lack of confidence, which ends in shame and doubt. She lacks confidence and courage and does not trust herself.

Forward says, "An important part of parenting process is gradually stepping back to let a little girl learn for herself and when a mother's control precludes her child from doing that, it ceases to be helpful and loving" (2014, 70). There is always a connection between being bullied at home as a young child and becoming vulnerable to bullying in the outside world, especially in school. When a child is pushed to be quiet, uncomplaining, and compliant by a controlling mother, this child will naturally take the route of being passive, essentially learning to be a target. When this individual grows up and chooses the religious life, she will continue to be compliant and passive, and this of course is translated as "very obedient," to the detriment of others who stand up for themselves.

The behaviors studied in this research are some of the ones that people with emotional turmoil exhibit. The findings in chapter 4 support the hypotheses.

*Hypothesis Number 3*

Building a strong inner world with proper emotional balance from childhood on is crucial to coping with life in a healthy manner as an adult.

For a child to have a strong inner world, the child must have felt loved, cared for, supported, and respected. A good-enough mother does not brush off or minimize a child's emotions. When children feel they can go to their parents when they need help, they feel supported and cared for. A strong inner world is one in which a person feels connected, cared for, and held. This is important for the building of inner strength, which helps a person calmly deal with whatever stressful situations come their way. It is inner fortitude. Some mothers "frequently withdraw into their own world, abandoning their role as caretakers. They may be home, but they're rarely present enough to notice your accomplishment or wipe away your tears after a disappointment. Instead, they spend their day sleeping, complaining. watching TV..." (Forward 2014, 87).

Proper emotional balance allows people to be aware of and recognize their emotions as they occur and how they impact their daily lives. An individual who has acquired this balance is compassionate, caring, supportive, respectful and loving toward others in the same environment, and able to calmly deal with situations that arise in their adult lives. Winnicott's capacity for concern (1990) is portrayed here. Erikson talks about parents providing a facilitating environment in which the child can learn and gain control, thus building self-esteem, but a rigid, harsh, demanding parent will break the child's confidence so the child will experience shame and doubt (1994). Winnicott discusses the capacity to imagine, and the good-enough mother needs to provide the holding environment so the growing child can gradually and creatively meet the world (1963). If a child has taken on the guilt and shame of her parents and the shame experienced in her own self-image and also internalized her mother's neglectful attitude, drunkenness, anger, and abuse, the child will not have any positive inner strength.

The findings regarding those who grew up with a father show that 77.18% selected "My father spent time listening to me and having conversation with me." The religious life has rigorous and challenging demands, from its prayer regimen to the observance of the three evangelical counsels (vows); therefore, persons choosing this way of life will need inner fortitude and proper emotional balance. A strong inner world can help people strengthen their outer world, and this is important for the religious life. From the research findings, "unable to handle crises" was commonly selected by both those who grew up with their fathers and those who did not. The hypothesis is confirmed.

### *Hypothesis Number 4*

Steady emotional growth in different stages of life parallel to physical growth contributes to the evolution of a mature person who has the capacity to make the right choices and decisions.

Erikson believed in step-by-step growth (1950). A person grows by steps or in stages, and in each of the stages, the individual confronts a task and masters it. Then she faces new challenges, and all these challenges need to be mastered for emotional health. So steady emotional growth is a uniform, consistent, dependable, and undisturbed pattern of a child's emotional maturing from one stage to another (Winnicott 1998; Erikson 1980). Children can accomplish this if they have parents who give them encouragement and praise; are positive role models; and teach them how to understand their emotions of anxiety, sadness, anger, frustration, and joy as well as how to handle them and express them in a healthy manner. In this way, children will grow to become mature adults. Of those who grew up with their fathers, 75.17% selected "My father encouraged me to do better when I made mistakes or fell short," and 93.96% selected "My father was a positive role model in my life." Maturity is a trait that is learned as a child in a nonthreatening environment (Winnicott 2005). So then, a mature person is one who is open minded, who has no mental wall to prevent her from seeing the world through the eyes of those with different ideas. A psychologically mature sister would be one who is able to step back from situations and evaluate them rationally instead of acting in the here and now and giving in to emotions. William James terms individuals who are religious and psychologically immature "sick souls" (1996). In religious life, most often other sisters' ideas are not welcomed, especially for those who find themselves in a diverse cultural environment. Rather, it is always survival of the fittest. Often, there is no dialogue, and a lot of ruthlessness comes into play. Discipline by shaming or controlling and being uninterested in what others feel are the order of the day, and they are some of the behaviors in the questionnaire. For those who did grow up with their fathers, discipline by shaming was rated as thus: Congregation, 56 (37.58%), Final profession 39 (26.17%), Temporal professed, 24 (16.11%), Novices, 24 (16.11%), Postulants, 13 (8.73%). Controlling: Congregation, 88 (59.06%), Final profession, 78 (52.33%), Temporal professing, 34 (22.82%), Novices, 14 (9.40%), Own behavior 29 (19.46%). Not interested in how others feel: Congregation, 60 (40.25%), Final professed 58 (35.90%), Own behavior 28 (18.75%). Turning to those who did not grow up with their fathers, Discipline by shaming: Congregation, 11 (37.93%), Final professed, 7 (24.14%), Temporal professed, 11 (37.93%), Novices, 7 (24.14%), postulants, 4 (13.79%) Own behavior, 10 (34.48%). Controlling: Congregation, 8 (27.59%), Final professed, 10 (34.48%), Own behavior, 7 (24.145). Not interested in what other's feel:

Congregation, 6 (20.69%), Final professed, 7 (24.14%), Temporal professed, 7 (24.14%), Novices, 6 (20.69%), Postulants, 7 (24.14%) Own behavior, 12 (41.38%).

Many have experienced the destructiveness, ruthlessness, and lack of compassion of other sisters as well as their leaders in the convent environment, without any form of reparation. Others, in order to protect themselves, have repaid these sisters with their own ruthlessness. It is important that religious women acknowledge their destructive tendencies and work toward containing them. This means there is a brokenness in each person's life that needs to be repaired. A lot of projective identification happens in religious houses. Projection-identification is a term that Melanie Klein introduced into psychoanalysis. It is "a defense mechanism in which an individual projects qualities that are unacceptable to the self onto another individual and that person," through unconscious interpersonal pressure, "internalizes the projected qualities and believes... herself to be characterized by them" *(APA Dictionary of Psychology 2006, 740)*. This situation leads sisters to become isolated and unhappy, thinking there must be something wrong with regard to the person identifying with the projections. If these women could care enough, they would be able to imagine how others experience their dark or destructive sides. People's inability to feel and own their destructive nature and make reparation is their lack of compassion and their lack of the capacity for concern -one of Winnicott's capacities. The ability for people to have this capacity stems from how strongly and consistently they were received by their holding environments. This hypothesis is confirmed.

**Hypotheses Number 5**

Positive validation is very important in the growth of a child as she builds a stronger self within that reflects later in life as an adult with a healthy self-esteem.

Of those who grew up with their fathers, 81.21% agreed with "My father encouraged me to do good at whatever I was doing." Similarly, 75.84% chose "My father was affectionate and playful with me," and 95.3% selected "My father supported and encouraged me to become a leader." Positive validation occurs when the primary caregiver provides positive feedback to the growing child. An acknowledgment of as well as appreciation of tasks that the child tries, performs, or accomplishes and shows initiative to complete is very important (Winnicott 1990; Erikson, 1980). Positive validation makes a child feel heard, seen, thought of, and appreciated for who she is (Winnicott 1965, 2005; and Erikson 1994). This launches a child's sense of self-worth that will follow her into adulthood. When a person comes to the religious life with a healthy self-esteem, it is evident in what she does and says. Healthy self-esteem reflects the overall emotional evaluation of one's worth. It reveals how a person feels about herself regardless of stress. The person believes "I am competent" or "I am worthy." She can manage disappointments or exciting events with ease. She can recognize her emotions but not allow them to rule her mood and tries to do things that will make her feel good. The other side of the coin is the lack of positive validation.

A lack of positive validation makes a child believe, for example, "I am not recognized, appreciated, thought of, or seen." This belief results in low self-esteem and diminishes self-confidence. When an individual enters the religious life, she brings what she has— feelings of guilt, helplessness, worthlessness, and insecurity; a lack of self-confidence or motivation; or a loss of identity or even an identity crisis. Of respondents who grew up with their fathers, 69.13% selected

"My father punished me when I made mistakes," and 28.19% agreed with "My father rebuked me publicly and shamed me when I made mistakes." Similarly, 26.10% to 32.89% indicated that they notice a lack of confidence in their respective environments. For those who did not grow up with their fathers, "suffers from mood swings" was one of the most commonly selected behaviors. Living in this type of environment is most often nothing to write home about. The hypothesis is confirmed.

### *Hypothesis Number 6*

In the choice of becoming a sister, an individual needs to possess a good, mature  psychological framework, within which is the key to live a happy and joyful religious life.

Basing our argument on the successful achievement of Winnicott's six capacities (1965), the individual will develop, possess, hold, and enjoy a healthy relationship with oneself, with others, and with the world, including others in the religious community. For Winnicott, this can come about through satisfactory parental care; and for Erikson, it results from the successful completion of his developmental stages (1994). In these developmental stages, the growing child must achieve the ego strength that goes with the task to avoid a core pathology in adulthood. For Erikson, this can happen when parents present consistent, adequate, is self-aware, accountable to others, and takes responsibility for her actions, even if she makes an error. Such people are eager to learn new things from others and broaden their horizons. When such an individual becomes a leader in the religious community, the prayers of the community members will be from the heart since the sisters will concentrate on God and not on how to be happy and fend for themselves physically and emotionally. Based on all this, the religious community becomes a home, a place where sisters are content, can pray earnestly and sincerely, and will be happy to seek God more, and apostolic life will flourish.

Psychological maturity grants people the ability to appropriately shift perspectives and gain an awareness of the big picture. Therefore, if children have not matured (grown up) psychologically and enter religious communities, there will be no dialogue, only rigidity. They would not appreciate differences of opinion or empower other members. They would not have enough time to complete functions or assignments, and they would consider a negative response from others to be an attack. They would have a diminished sense of personal sin. They would discipline others by shaming them and be able to keep confidence (American Behavioral Clinics 2021). They would rarely engage their inner critics or seek solitude. Religious communities would become places of fear, intimidation, and chaos. Following are some of the behaviors that were chosen by respondents as ones they have engaged in themselves. Among those who grew up with their fathers, "untrusting" was chosen by 20.81%; "tends to very angry" by 16.78%; "low self-esteem" by 20.81%; "anxious" by 44.30%; "trust issues" by 36.91%; "too sensitive" by 34.91%; and "gives up too easily" by 36.91%. Among those who did not grow up with their fathers, "untrusting" was selected by 34.48%; "difficulty in making and keeping friends" by 44.83%; "tends to be overly defensive" by 43.48%; "recognition seeking" by 44.83%; "self-blaming" by 37.93%; "trust issues" by 41.38%; "unable to handle crises" by 51.72%; "fear of being involved" by 41.38%; "too passive" by 48.28%; and "unable to handle one's emotions" by 41.38%. The findings support the hypothesis.

**Hypotheses Number 7**

A father's lack of emotional support for his growing child will make the child feel abandoned throughout her life.

Emotional support in childhood is provided when, for example, a parent lends a helping hand to a child in times of emotional discomfort or distress. Emotional support is important because it helps a child sense her place in the world, especially in her social, emotional, and cognitive development and functioning. It can shape the child into the person she becomes. A father's emotional support goes further to support the pregnant woman's adaptation to the pregnancy. A child looks to the father to provide a feeling of security, both physical and emotional.

When a father is involved in his child's life (Winnicott 1990), the child develops inner strength, which is a contributing factor to the outcome of inner sense of well-being and self-confidence. A female patient the researcher worked with frequently cried, "Why can't my father love me?" The father-daughter relationship is important because daughters depend on their fathers for security and emotional support. A loving and gentle father will influence his daughter to look for such goodness in men in her adult life. According to Kast, "Qualities and characteristics which have been experienced through the father are transferred to a male friend or to intellectual pursuit" (1997, 11). Kalsched adds, "A child is unable to hate a loved parent and instead identifies with the father as 'good' and through a process which Sandor Ferenczi called 'identification with the aggressor' the child takes the father's aggression into the inner world and comes to hate itself and its own need" (1996, 17). It is therefore, critical that the child receive positive emotional support. to look for such goodness in men in her adult life. According to Kast, "Qualities and characteristics which have been experienced through the father are transferred to a male friend or to intellectual pursuit" (1997, 11). Kalsched adds, "A child is unable to hate a loved parent and instead identifies with the father as 'good' and through a process which Sandor Ferenczi called 'identification with the aggressor' the child takes the father's aggression into the inner world and comes to hate itself and its own need" (1996, 17). It is therefore, critical that the child receive positive emotional support.

The following is an experience from the researcher's clinical work. A patient has one sibling, a male, and she is the only to look for such goodness in men in her adult life. According to Kast, "Qualities and characteristics which have been experienced through the father are transferred to a male friend or to intellectual pursuit" (1997, 11). Kalsched adds, "A child is unable to hate a loved parent and instead identifies with the father as 'good' and through a process which Sandor Ferenczi called 'identification with the aggressor' the child takes the father's aggression into the inner world and comes to hate itself and its own need" (1996, 17). It is therefore, critical that the child receive positive emotional support.

The following is an experience from the researcher's clinical work. A patient has one sibling, a male, and she is the only daughter of the family. She was very close to her father. Father and daughter admired each other, and her father had shown this publicly, identifying her as "Daddy's girl." There had always been competition between mother and daughter, and this had led to fights between them, in which the father always stood by his daughter. The patient acknowledged that she was only happy when she was the first in her father's affection and created situations to help her reclaim that. She recalled that, as a child, when she saw that her parents were getting closer without they including her, she cried and drew attention to herself. This led to disruption in the mother-daughter relationship and chaos in the family as well. Now as an adult, she has issues with her relationships. Kast explains that "such women need the admiration of men to preserve their self-esteem.... They become dependent on those who value them. Losing them means losing this self- esteem" (1995, 113).

A good father-daughter relationship is always influenced by the father's positive relationship with his own mother. A father may want a male child during the pregnancy, and if he instead gets a female child, accepts her, but does not spend much time with her as she grows up, she may internalize the way her father thinks and reasons so she will be accepted. Lack of emotional support for a child starts when parents fail to respond enough to a child's emotional needs while the child is being raised. Adults who feel abandoned may have experienced neglect, abuse, abandonment, and trauma during their childhoods, and they may repeat this behavior with their own children. As adults, they have abandonment issues (feelings of fear of losing or going to lose something), trust issues, (fear of being abandoned by others), and communication and relationship issues. They experience lots of guilt, shame and anger, depression, lack of compassion for themselves, and fear of being alone.

These people cycle through relationships, sabotaging the ones they truly desire, clinging to unhealthy relationships, and needing constant assurance. All this is some of the manifestation of borderline personality disorder symptoms, which is a byproduct of a deficit of emotional support. The repercussions of this behavior will affect all the other nuns or sisters in the religious community if this person happens to choose the religious life. In religious communities, the risky behavior of a borderline leader or superior is manifested in letting go of (expelling) sisters at random, and at the least provocation, even if it is just a day before they make their vows, which happens most of the time. A father's function is to help the child find a way out of the close symbiotic relationship between mother and child. A child who is "assured of interest and understanding, who is given love, care, sympathy and protection, will develop a healthy ego activity" (Kast 1997, 5). When we allow ourselves to be controlled by others, we steer away from our own developmental needs.

From the findings discussed in chapter 4, it is evident that many of the behaviors are very alive in the religious communities. Those who did not grow up with their fathers experience these behaviors: "difficulty in making and keeping friends," "untrusting," "anxious," "tend to be needy," "talks too much and listens too little," "gets sad/depressed easily and often," and "inability to control one's emotions."

"Difficulty making and keeping friends": Congregation 41.38%, Temporal professed 55.17%, Novices 51.72%, Postulants 44.83%, Own behavior 34.48%. "Tends to be needy": Congregation 44.83%, Final professed 34.48%, Temporal professed 68.97%, Novices 75.86%, Postulants 82.76%, Own 37.93%. "Talks too much and listens too little": Congregation 51.72%, Final professed 51.72%, Temporal professed 31.03%, Novices 34.48%, Postulants 24.14%, Own 41.38%. Interestingly, "gets sad/depressed easily and often" was rated high for Temporal professed 58.62% and Postulants 65.52%. "Inability to control one's emotions" was also rated high: Congregation 51.72%, Final professed 37.93%, Temporal professed 44.83%, Novices 48.28%, Postulants 62.07%, and Own 41.38%. "Untrusting": Congregation 44.83%, Final professed 39.93%, Temporal professed 65.52%, Novices 51.72%, Postulants 44.83%, and Own behavior 34.48%. "Anxious": Congregation 44.83%, Final professed 34.48%, Temporal professed 72.41%, Novices 44.83%, Postulants 44.83%, and Own behavior 20.69%.

## Observations and Discrepancies

The researcher observed some discrepancies or disconnections in the way the respondents who grew up with their fathers answered the questions. Respondents indicated on the first part of the questionnaire that they had good relationships with their fathers, yet they later indicated that they exhibit many of the adverse behaviors, like "untrusting," "tends to be needy," "anxious," "recognition seeking," "feelings of being ridiculed," "tends to get into other people's stuff," "trust issues," "unable to handle crises," "paranoid," "fear of rejection," "fear of getting involved," "suffer from mood swings," "too sensitive," "likes to fix other people's problems," "talks too much and listens too little," "fear of rejection," "controlling," and "lacks leadership skills." On one hand, they say they have warm, fuzzy relationships with their fathers, but on the other hand, these are the behaviors that resulted. There is a disconnect between these. Another disconnect is that most of the respondents have been professed for more than forty years and indicate warm, fuzzy relationships with their fathers, but they grew up in a time when fathers were not normally very involved with their children, even less so their female children. How could this be? They described what normally takes place now and not necessarily what went on in that era or when they were growing up. These respondents are sixty years of age and older presently.

It is interesting to note that none of the religious communities allowed their postulants to participate in the study. Maybe they were concerned that the postulants would describe them negatively since they know them very well. They never gave reasons, but I have been wondering what made them exclude the candidates and postulants from participating while the rest of the respondents were able to rate postulants' behaviors. Another interesting observation is how common certain behaviors were among the congregations, including "controlling," 59.06%; "untrusting," 55%; "tends to be needy," 51.68%; "tends to get into other people's stuff," 51.01%; "trust issues," 55.03%; "anxious," 42.95%; "tends to be overly defensive," 40.27%; "too sensitive," 48.32%; and "talks too much and listens too little," 53.69%. In addition, even though many respondents said they had good relationships with their fathers, 47.65% of them selected "My father tried to control what I did and how I did it."

From the findings, we can say that these hypotheses have been proven to be true, and the presentation in chapter 4 demonstrates that.

*Chapter 6*

# Overview of the study?

This has been a very comprehensive study. The main object and purpose of this study was to look critically at what a person who has chosen to respond to the call brings to the religious life and how people's histories and past experiences influence the choices they make. Many of the behaviors exhibited by those in religious-life environments and communities are not talked about but are known, either because people do not know what to do about them or because people are in denial that these need to be addressed. Most often, prayer is what is stressed in these environments. It is a known fact that it is not easy for a person in formation or training (temporal professed, novices, and postulants) to speak openly against these behaviors for fear of being let go (expelled), so they have been accepted as the norm with the hope that prayers could solve the situation. The researcher remembers her own training, when "impure thoughts" were stressed constantly. She remembers asking her instructor one day, "Sister, what are these impure thoughts you always talk about?"

The researcher's hope was for the director to address the infighting and other disruptive behaviors surrounding them that disturbed the peace of the convent, but that did not happen.

Some of the causes of these behavior patterns have been carefully investigated by the researcher. The researcher studied non variables in their own setting. Because of this, a simple survey design was used in the selected religious congregations. Sampling was done to obtain a representative sample of the population from which information on the entire population of people in religious life could be obtained. A questionnaire and a group process designed by the researcher were used to collect the needed information.

The study makes it clear that these behaviors exist in all religious communities, and they not only disrupt the smooth running of the communities' affairs but also bring social and spiritual chaos, which lead to spiritual stagnation. This is manifested in the sisters' attitudes toward prayer life, work, various apostolates, and decision-making processes.

**Group Process**

The researcher formed a small group to augment the unanswered questions. The group process exists to help people grow emotionally and to solve personal problems. Permission was obtained by the researcher to use a space for the group-process meeting via phone. Before the phone conversation and permission, the researcher visited a community chapel two times and shared with individual sisters her research topic. Twenty sisters from different religious groups were selected and invited to attend the four sessions. The researcher made personal phone calls to thank those who agreed to be part of the meetings. Participants expressed gratitude for the researcher's interest in behavioral issues. The group met four times. All sessions were held after morning services on Sundays, with each session lasting sixty minutes. Ten minutes were used for introduction and ten minutes for coffee and doughnuts. Music by Mozart was played following the refreshments to put the participants in a prayerful frame of mind. After that, the group went straight to reviewing and discussing the questions. Some rules were established for the group, which participants tried to obey.

The rules are as follows:

1. Anything heard in the group stays in the group.

2. Respect what another person says.

3. We want to respect each person's need to be heard.

4. We listen when another is speaking.

5.  We want to explore new ideas and explain our feelings

6. We will not be judgmental.


All groups were willing and eager to answer the questions. They were open and answered the questions with sincerity. After the music and the explanation of the purpose of the research, the participants were given the questionnaire. Open discussions were held before they filled out the questionnaire regarding experiences participants had encountered as they relate to their community living. The researcher's role in the group was to facilitate individuals' efforts to express their feelings and freely communicate their experiences. The group process was relevant to this research because it is an interaction of people appreciating one another in gradual, facilitated conversation about issues participants have not felt free to talk about. The researcher used Irvin D. Yalom's eleven curative factors, which he identified as the primary agents of change in his book *The Theory and Practice of Group Psychotherapy* (1995). In the group interactions, these eleven curative factors manifested themselves. Briefly, these eleven curative factors that are the primary agents of change are as follows:

1. Installation of hope

2.  Universality

3. Imparting information

4. Altruism

5. The corrective recapitulation of the primary family group

6. Development of the socializing technique

7. Imitative behavior

8. Interpersonal learning

9. Group cohesiveness

10. Catharsis

11. Existential factors

In terms of these factors, the researcher made some observations of the group participants:

**Installation of Hope**

The participants (sisters) came to this group hoping to share, learn and decrease the pain, shame, and isolation they have experienced in their religious orders. The researcher's role as a psychoanalyst was to acknowledge the presence of each participant so she would feel listened to and would herself listen attentively to others as they shared or expressed how they had faced their setbacks and problems. The experiences of others instilled hope in others; it helped to know that someone else truly understood what goes on in this environment. Comments like "I thought I was the only one" gave hope to others.

**Universality**

The group of twenty participants from different religious orders showed that these behavioral patterns are universal in all religious societies. One person said that she had thought that her congregation's situation was unique, but upon hearing others, she felt a common bond.

## Imparting Information

Based on the information that factual knowledge changes attitudes and relieves uncertainties and confusion, the researcher provided information about the project under stdy and suggestions to help the participants in the group deal with the bottled-up pain and unresolved emotional issues. By sharing that information, it became clear that the participants' motivations to join the different orders varied. Confidentiality was emphasized as the group gathered to share stories of pain and shame.

## Altruism

This is a selfless concern for the welfare of others outside of one's own environment. The researcher and the participants are all sisters. The sisters were there for one another. They were empathetic and offered support, reassurance, and insights. The participants understood the problems but felt they could not do anything about them.

## The Corrective Recapitulation of the Primary Group

The families of origin's experiences influenced the interpersonal relationships among these group members. Authority and parental figure influences, deep emotions, and hostility were buried deep in the participants. In simple terms, the researcher referenced some old, unresolved family issues within the group without having a particular target.

## Development of Socializing Technique

Yalom asserts that social learning, or the development of basic social skills, is a therapeutic factor that occurs in all groups (1995). The sisters offered feedback to one another about the appropriateness of how they have handled their pain and how they also have been a source of pain to others. Through the development of social skills, they learned to be less judgmental and resolved to learn the skills to resolve their own conflicts.

## Imitative Behavior

Yalom believes that groups allow people to try behaviors they have witnessed in others (1995). For example, children learn by imitation. In the second meeting, the participants shared a lot of positive feedback, which enhanced self-esteem and emotional growth. The participants were more cordial and more poised in action, speech, and dress, as if they were competing with one another.

## Interpersonal Learning

Human beings are interrelated. Interpersonal learning leads to transformation of unwanted pattern of behaviors. Even though the group did not meet for long, some participants expressed gratitude for the empowerment they had learned and the ability to open up. They reported that they learned that their emotions were real and legitimate and that they could do something about them; it was up to them. The supportive environment created during the encounter encouraged participants to look for more ways to share their emotions. Sharing openly motivated some to offer their own perspectives and honest feedback. The outcome was to interact and share more deeply and honestly.

## Group Cohesiveness

Every human being wants to be accepted and feel that he or she belongs. The first thing the researcher did was to connect herself to the group. Group encounters can be a powerful healing factor as individuals replace their feelings of loneliness and anger with a sense of belonging and acceptance. Cohesive groups allow greater expression of all emotions, including hostility toward other group members and even the facilitator. As an analyst, the researcher is aware that unexpressed hostility leads to resentment and that decreased cohesiveness reduces the chances of conflict resolution and personal growth. Researcher did her best to contain any conflict, especially if one person dominated the discussion or someone spoke at random, to keep the group communication open. Participants learned that everyone's perspective is valued, and so as a group learned to be less afraid and opened up

## Catharsis

Catharsis is a type of learning (as opposed to intellectual understanding) that can lead to immediate opportunity for people to have a powerful experience. It is emotional ventilation. The participants let out bottled-up emotions by talking about their hurt and unheard life stories. Some participants talked out of turn, but they learned that the group accepted even that. Catharsis cannot be imposed on a group. This group environment provided ample opportunity for members to have these powerful experiences. The group met after church services.

## Existential Factors

Certain realities of life affect humans. These include the families we are born into, isolation, freedom, and the meaninglessness of life and death. Awareness of these facts sometimes causes anxiety, which is very natural. The trust and openness that developed among the religious sisters or nuns permitted the exploration of these fundamental issues. The end result was that the participants developed an acceptance of these realities. After the encounter, these ideas or themes came up:

1. How do we address these behavioral issues in our orders since they are so broad?

2. How do we learn to take more responsibility for our actions in our different orders?

3. How do we develop empathy toward others in the same environment?

During the encounters with the participants, the researcher discovered that her emotional presence was valued more than her skills and knowledge. Some of the participants expressed that they will be supportive of fellow sisters in their various communities. They were happy to observe their three evangelical counsels of poverty, chastity, and obedience, but their concerns were that they would be treated well by others in the community and the behavioral issues would be dealt with.

**Surprise Outcome Not Anticipated**

The participants were able to express more opinions than those who answered the questionnaire. Since they did not previously know the researcher well, their readiness to discuss the items on the questionnaire as well as the behaviors existing in the communities was surprising. They spoke readily and discussed some painful situations they had experienced themselves. At first, there was a high level of denial that their societies or communities had any issues, but later they opened up. According to the APA Dictionary of Psychology, denial is a defense mechanism in which unpleasant thoughts, feelings, and events are ignored or excluded from the conscious awareness (2006). It may take the form of a refusal to acknowledge reality. "Denial is an unconscious process that functions to resolve emotional conflicts or reduce anxiety" *(APA Dictionary of Psychology 2006, 268)*. As the researcher discovered in her study of family dynamics, the participants were denying the fact

158

that serious behavioral issues existed and that they had been victims of abuse. The researcher shared some insights from the research with the sisters.

Resistance was also observed. When in therapy a client is resistant, for example, the individual is likely fearful, anxious, embarrassed, shameful, or helpless. This person may fear that the therapist, counselor, or group as a whole will treat her in a hurtful manner. Nicholas says, "Minuchin's solution to the problem of resistance is straight forward. He wins families over by joining and accommodating them. This gives him the leverage to utilize powerful confrontations designed to restructure family interaction. Resistance is seen as a product of the interactions between the family and therapist. Change is accomplished by alternatively challenging the family and then rejoining them to repair breaches in the therapeutic relationship" (2004, 384). The researcher practiced Minuchin's solution by being empathetic to the group members, representing different religious orders, having heard all they had to encounter and live with in their congregations. She achieved this through nonreactions-not expressing coercion, anger, or intolerance to their resistance during the sharing. These basic skills assisted in the interpretation of the participants' resistance by identifying and discussing unspoken feelings.

This is a story of how one person's true self was threatened and diminished in her religious community. She was a young sister, two years temporal professed, when she was assigned to a community to teach in a newly established high school. She had a great imagination and could write plays and then get schoolchildren to act them out. The plays were always acted in the church. The church members loved the plays because they gave them a reason to be out of their homes and meet other Church members. When she was in the novitiate (training center, training to become a sister), she wrote a play that was acted out by the catechumens (those preparing for baptism, Holy Communion, and confirmation) for the entire church. It was a great success. The director asked her to write another play for the novices (those in training with her), so she did, and the novices acted it out. The novice director at that time invited church members to watch the play. It was also successful. As a temporal professed sister teaching in the high school, she brought up the idea of the students' acting out a play to bring the school into the public eye, and the principal, who also happened to be the superior or leader of the sister's community, agreed. The students were excited and put a lot of energy into the practice and memorization of lines, meeting in person for the practices. After regular weekly practices for three months, all were set for the acting of the play (stage and others). The bishop of the area had invited chiefs and other important dignitaries to attend the play. However, the day before the play was scheduled, her principal and superior told her, "You little girl, you have become so popular and have taken away my glory. You cannot put on the play." And so, the play was canceled.

The bishop could not take the shame and so wrote an SOS letter to the general superior of the congregation requesting a meeting. The religious sister added that she felt so ashamed and humiliated that she lost interest in writing plays. Her imaginative capacity died that day. That part of her was gone forever. All the participants were moved by the story. Interestingly, the researcher in her own life had encountered a situation that, instead of diminishing her, invigorated and transformed her. The researcher understood her defenses and experienced a new level of emotional and psychological maturity. Below is the researcher's experience. "By emotional maturity we mean the ability to control ... anxiety, withstand stress, and maintain balance during times of change" (Chapman and Campbell 2005, 142).

## The Researcher's Own Transformational Experience

To have a philosophy of life is a good thing because it could serve as a guiding principle to follow. The word *philosophy* is derived from the Greek words *philos*, meaning "loving," and Sophia, meaning "wisdom " — so it is the love of wisdom. Philosophy has many definitions according to Titus, Smith, and Nolan (1979). In their book *Living Issues in Philosophy*, they attempted to give five definitions, but for my own purpose I am using two of them. First, philosophy "is a set of attitudes or beliefs towards life and the universe which are often held uncritically" (Titus et al. 1979, 10). This is the meaning when people say, "This is my philosophy." Second, "philosophy is a process of reflecting upon and criticizing our most deeply held beliefs and attitudes" (Titus et al. 1979, 10). These definitions have helped me to take a second look at my interactions and relational styles as a person. They have helped me think through a variety of problems presented to me as a young religious woman and those in my analytical sessions. My philosophy has challenged my belief system and clarified things for me. My view of the human person is that everyone is created in the image and likeness of God; as such, each person has dignity (Gen 1:27). For this reason, each person is a child of God. Each person created has the dignity to be able to live and reach to his or her potential. Since all humans are created in the image and likeness of God, all are equal in the eyes of God and have the freedom to live. No one is superior to another. We have the same basic nature. This equality of the dignity of humans motivated my desire to take this journey of transformation.

Hope was very present in my journey of transformation. Hope is to wish for something with expectation for its fulfillment. Hope is an emotion characterized by the sense that one will have a positive experience. It is a belief that one can influence the experience in a positive way. Hope fuels my faith.

Hope gives me openness to what is possible. It opens me to thepossibility of what I anticipate-health and wholeness.

My own journey of transformation began more than thirty years ago when I was in an international, multicultural, and racially diverse religious group. Coming from a place where all was not settled with regard to antagonistic tribal attitudes, I had to embrace this journey that brought a major shift in my thinking about the people of the Northern part of the Country to whom I was to minister. Culture is all around us, shaping our behavior, and people from various cultures will process the world differently. Many generations earlier, these people from the North were used as house help, working for the people of the Southern part of the Country without proper compensation. These days, work like this is compensated. I had felt dissatisfaction about the recruitment of young women into my society in my province, questioning why Southerners could enter our community more readily than Northerners. No compelling answer was offered. I felt this inner call to journey to the North, out of my comfort zone, to recruit young women from that area. I was traveling to the unknown; I had never been to this part of the country before. I was to encounter my own self. "The journey is from the realm of limitation to a world wide open to unlimited possibility. The hero must discover rituals and ceremonies, rites of passages that allow access to the threshold between these worlds" (Hartman and Zimberoff 2009, 4). Racial issues were a part of this journey.

In the book *The Multicultural Imagination: "Race," Color, and the Unconscious,* Adams states, "Racism is any characterization of people on the basis of physical characteristics, for example, skin color" (1996). However, skin color was not the problem in this part of the world, but racism on the basis of one's ancestors and from where they originated.

These people of the North have accepted the fact that they are poor, and the people of the South have assumed the role of superior and rich. One's perception affects one's thinking and behavior.

Altman states that "aggression, sexuality, criminality, and exploitation are often disowned by people of relatively high social status and projected onto... those of lower social status. People of lower social status may disown intelligence and ambition and project these qualities onto those of higher status" (1995, 83). This social class system brings about low or high self-esteem, depending on which side one takes. This is what Altman calls "the hidden injuries of class" (1995, 83). Even though times have changed, these superiority and inferiority complexes still exist. All the while I had thought that my being a religious individual would automatically erase these racial issues. I was naive. It became clear to me that this class prejudice has to be dealt with and from within. This is what the hero had to go through. "The hero encounters a guardian" on the journey, according to Hartman and Zimberoff (2009, 4). Another sister's parents were from the North but had migrated to the South as children, grown up there, and married, meaning this sister was born and educated in the South. She offered to be my companion on the journey, understanding well what I would be facing. Her support gave me the courage to go through all the stages of the journey.

I could not meet with anyone until I had met with the bishop. Arrangements had already been made, and he was aware of my arrival. And I was aware of this collective underpinning reality of the North and South class issue. The information we acquire from our interpretations results in a change. It alters how we see or think about certain subjects. This class issue is not openly talked about, but it is acted out unconsciously, thus bringing out the hidden injuries of the class system. When I finally met with the bishop, he told me, "You Southerners do not respect the Northerners. You have come to recruit girls to join your order. You will not get any of our girls." He added, "If you get even three of our girls, I will build a convent for your society in my diocese." I could hear the contempt in his voice. He met me with his vicar and two priests. Lots of young women were joining the diocesan congregation the bishop had started in the North (*diocesan* meant they would work only for the bishop and his diocese), while fewer girls or young women were joining congregations from the South. I feel we are all equal, and since I was already there, I decided to "claim the treasure hard to attain"-get some girls from the North to join my order. This is one of the stages of the hero's journey. I had to go through the "land of the unknown." I traveled for the whole day and night on a very muddy, untarred road. I felt tired, sick, and hungry. My skin felt sticky. I threw up at least twice. (The roads are excellent now.) When I reached my destination, I struggled to eat the food and drink that was set before me. I could not eat. It was very different from what I was used to. I asked myself whether it was a bad decision to have made this journey. I felt hungry and defeated. I noticed something, though. The older women who cooked for me were very nice and very respectful. Like the hero in Marie-Louise von Franz's book *The Interpretation of Fairy Tales*, I met difficulties. Von Franz stated, "In difficult times like these the ego adopts a heroic, courageous and hopeful attitude that saves the collective situation" (1996, 63). It was left for me to go through the challenge to bridge the split between the North and the South in myself. This journey was one of transformation of my defenses, biases, and prejudices inherited from many generations. Research has shown that biases affect our ability to judge correctly, our perception, and our judgment as well. Biased thinking leads to misunderstanding, wrong decisions, and costly consequences and mistakes.

I learned to eat their food and drink their locally made wine, and I interacted with the people as well. I did enjoy the food set before me. This was the beginning of bridging thegap between the North and the South in my community. I was able to visit all the Catholic high schools in the North in the company of a priest who offered to drive me to all of them since I had arrived on public transportation. After this massive tour, ten young women joined our society. It was the joy of everyone. We do not consider the young women Northerners. Instead, we address them as "our sisters."

Basch says, "In a successful treatment, the patient learns to perceive himself differently" (1980, 36). I have learned to perceive myself differently, not as superior to but the same as the women from the North. For me, the split has disappeared. I had to sacrifice and lay myself bare to redeem myself and my perception of the North if I intended to be a good vocation promoter for the entire country. The bishop who said he would build a convent if I recruited even three of his girls saw that I had more than ten at the very beginning, so he built not one but four convents or homes for the congregation to live in and minister to the people in health care and education. The first ten have had their silver jubilees.

I had internalized the idea that Southerner are superior to Northerners, and these internalized feelings would not be helpful if I had to recruit people from the whole country. This helped me recast my life's story. I went on a journey of psychological freedom. I went through a psychological change and a cultural shift, which brought a social shift and change in my life. This cultural shift is reflected in my belief that all people are equal, regardless of their place of origin. This shift made me look at this question: What makes one a person? Jung describes individuation as a "process by which a person becomes a psychological 'in-dividual' ... a separate, indivisible unity or whole" (1990, 275). The psychological journey brings transformation. The individual becomes whole, unity, cohesive, or integrated. My own journey of hope and transformation happened when I met the "other" who journeyed with me. Jung adds, "An ego may be present, but it cannot experience its wholeness within the framework of its own personality.... It is still in the stage of unconscious identification with the plurality of the group" (1990, 275). I had to become my own hero. I could not stay in my safe zone. I had to reach into the space of the "other." The intersubjective space brings healing. The journey was "I am superior," and it initiated me into a new world of "we are all created in the image and likeness of God: therefore, we are equal." This was a journey of becoming my own authentic self. The hero's journey was made more readily available to me as was elaborated by Jung in his book *Symbol of Transformation.*

He states that, in the hero's journey of transformation, the hero can integrate the previously hidden and unknown depths of the self into consciousness. The journey is about confronting one's shadows and jumping over all the hurdles to reach wholeness. "The self (soul) is so powerful, so determined to become wholly conscious, that it continually haunts and prods us" (Hartman and Zimberoff 2009, 6). They add, "The hero is that part of us that says, 'yes' to life, that embraces life's challenges and that always wants to grow, improve and contribute even at the cost of going through hell" (12). In the journey, I encountered myself. The hero's journey of transformation continues as we continue to live life.

As I discovered from the participants in the group encounters, a young woman faces serious situations when she first visits the sisters in the "come and see" program that are not normally talked about. Most of them have very traumatic feelings of shock, numbness, sadness, anger, guilt, anxiety, and fear. The director of vocations who invited the women in the first place may not even acknowledge these situations, not to mention the attitudes and behaviors of the other members of the community the visitor meets.

## Educational Implication of the Study

Notwithstanding the fact that the use of questionnaires in studies of this nature usually introduces shortcomings, some conclusions have been made based on the findings. This study created an awareness that these disruptive behaviors exist in all religious communities because women come to the convent with who they are and what they have. Erikson says that we as people are impacted greatly by the families and societies that welcomed us (identity and the life cycle); and Winnicott, in his book *Home Is Where We Start From,* explains how our home experiences create healthy or unhealthy personalities. This study attempts to show that it is okay to acknowledge who we are and choose to do something about it because none of us choose the homes in which we find ourselves.

The study also provides an awareness that being a religious sister or nun does not mean we have no right to be happy and fulfilled. We have a right to become the image of God we were created to be. This can only happen if we look inward. In all of us, there is a sacred garden "where the soul" abides and where the "transcendent reality" lives, "the sacred core" (Pargament 2007, 32). In his book *Counseling for Spiritually Empowered Wholeness,* Clinebell states, "Growing persons are moving toward increasing acceptance of and openness to themselves and others; growing awareness of and respect for reality; increasing self-support and self-esteem... growing capacity to give and receive love... greater freshness of perception of richness of feelings (both joy and pains)" (1995, 3-4).

The study challenges us to begin to look critically at and recognize the relationship between our childhoods, our life experiences, and the call to the religious life and ministry. Alice Miller, in her book *Thou Shall Not Be Aware* says, "The key to understanding the present situation lies in the past" (1998, 198). The compliant false self that allowed itself to be manipulated will need to be awakened so that the true self will prevail. It may be hard, but it's achievable. "For it is only through risk taking... that growth can occur" (Allport 1955, 66). As religious women, repairing a broken relationship is important, as are giving a warm smile, affirming the goodness in another person, expressing compassion and empathy, loving our sisters in community-all are signs of maturity. Leaders of communities need to invite others into their decision-making processes, and even though it may take a long time, the leaders will eventually find themselves conforming in ways they could not have imagined—thus creating the ability for them to listen as well.

**Recruitment Implication of the Study**

This research study on behaviors that are prevalent in religious communities opens a vast world of research. It is a way to challenge leaders of these religious communities to seek transformation of self. This transformation needs to be done through education on who one is as a mature adult. Formators should consider being formed themselves by understanding how their own attachments styles (threatened or related) and life experiences can influence the relationships they have with those in formation. These formators need to have the courage to investigate their own depths psychologically instead of the surfaces of their lives. Since the behavior of an individual is the product of the individual's perception, it is important for religious leaders and formators to understand not only their own perceptions but also those of the sisters in their care so they can create situations under which their behavior might improve.

Miller states, "If an individual begins to discover the truth about his early childhood and free himself from the internalized taboos and compulsions of his upbringing, including those of his introjects...those around him will benefit" (1984, 197-198). Formators will need to cry with those who cry and laugh with those who laugh. This is Winnicott's capacity for concern, which is much needed in the various religious communities. When formators are duly transformed to reach their potentials they will be able to impart their wisdom to the candidates coming to join them. Without first integrating love and hate in our own person, those we serve will experience us as ruthless and aloof, emotionally disconnected from our own issues and from their problems.

**Behavioral Implication of the Study**

It is important to look at the behavioral implication of the study with regard to Erikson's eight stages of psychosocial development as well as Winnicott's six capacities. The behavioral implication of the study will point toward how the individual chooses to behave as a religious sister or how a group of religious sisters behaves in any given situation, whether it be in their social relationships, at school, at a hospital, or in their own religious institutions. Wherever they are, they have to exhibit emotional self- regulation, executive functioning, creativity, and even a capacity to be alone. The capacity to be alone, a construct put forth by Winnicott (1958, 1974), is an internalization of the presence of the good-enough caregiver (Winnicott 1962, 1965), who is reliable and constant. This internalization engenders in the child an ability to tolerate anxiety, thus enabling a child to play and create. In the same vein, sisters in a religious congregation have to learn to tolerate anxiety and to create if they have learned to internalize a good-enough mother.

When an infant does not have a dependable caregiver, or when a once-stable caregiver becomes inconsistent, the infant's capacity to be alone is not engendered or is lost. In the same way, when a postulant or a novice does not have a dependable novice mistress or director, she can become a lost soul in the convent. She may stop thriving in her vocation.

The ability to be alone originates, paradoxically, in a relationship—the original relationship between the parent, usually the mother, and the infant. It is this relationship that provides, as Winnicott states, the "potential space between (what was at first) baby and mother-figure, with the baby in a state of near-absolute dependence, and the mother-figure's adaptive function taken for granted by the baby" (1968/2001a, 51-52). It is within this potential space that the infant finds objects-more accurately, the infant believes that she generates objects (e.g., a toy, a blanket, mother's voice, the infant's fingers) --that facilitate the growth of the infant's potential to experience and convey her true self (Winnicott 1960/1974b). Just like there is a potential space between the baby and the mother and where the baby is in a state of absolute dependence, so also the young sisters or nuns manifest their dependency on the sister superior and the community. Just as the infant finds objects to feel the connectedness, so do the young sisters find their connectedness with some objects like the rosary beads, the chapel, the Holy Eucharist, the voice of the good-role-model sisters, and the recreational activities in the community.

"Playing is itself a therapy," Winnicott asserts, in what has now become a famous turn of phrase from Playing and Reality (1971, 50). This commendation of play marks a milestone in psychoanalysis. According to him, "To arrange for children to be able to play is itself a psychotherapy that has immediate and universal application, and it includes the establishment of a positive social attitude towards playing"

(Winnicott 1971, 50). Playing, which cannot be dissociated from creativity and a sense of enjoyment, is an intensely real experience that has intrinsic therapeutic virtue, that is to say it is capable of promoting self-healing. So also, in the community, either indoor or outdoor play will become therapeutic to the individual sisters who participate in it. That is why the superiors also should understand the importance of recreation time for the community. Without imagination they cannot play. Without creativity they will have a life full of stagnation (Erikson/ Winnicott).

According to Winnicott, an unconscious process occurs within an ordinary mother who is fond of her baby (1952): she is the good-enough mother, who learns best how to look after her baby not from health professionals and self-help books but from having been a baby herself. She acts naturally (Winnicott 1988). Winnicott suggests that, during pregnancy, a mother develops a state of heightened sensitivity that continues to be maintained for some weeks after the baby's birth. When this heightened state passes, the mother has what Winnicott calls a flight into sanity, and she begins to be aware of the world that exists outside of her state of primary maternal preoccupation with her infant (Winnicott 1975). Nonetheless, the good-enough mother continues to provide an environment that facilitates healthy maturational processes in her baby. She achieves this by being the person who wards off the unpredictable and who actively provides care in the holding, handling, and general management of the child. The good- enough mother provides physical care and meets her baby's needs for emotional warmth and love.

In religious congregations, something similar needs to happen. A religious vocation needs to be nurtured. The sister in charge or vocation director and the formation team have to be good-enough mothers to facilitate healthy maturational processes in aspirants, postulants, and novices who are new to the life trying to reflect, focus, and answer the call of God. These young people are trying to fathom the meaning of this call and are looking for support and a good holding environment where their vocation can thrive. When sisters do not achieve the psychosocial stages of Erikson, they become untrusting of other sisters. They have doubts even about their call.

Furthermore, Winnicott observed ininfants the gradual formation of the self, a self that can have an experience that is real. For a religious sister to achieve this, she must develop and possess the six capacities proposed by Winnicott. She must also work to resolve all the psychosocial fixations incurred in each stage of Erikson's theory in order to hold and enjoy a healthy relationship with herself, with others, and with the world. The absence of these abilities coupled with fixations in some of Erickson's stages of growth and development leaves the sister deprived, and the consequence is clear in the various dysfunctional behaviors exhibited by the affected persons. Such include but are not limited to "untrusting," "difficulty in making and keeping friends," "tends to be angry most of the time," "tends to be needy," "tends to be overly defensive," "recognition seeking," "self-blaming," "anxious," "low self-esteem," "feelings of being ridiculed," "tends to get into other people's stuff," "discipline or retaliating by shaming," "feelings of loneliness," "fear of being judged," "feelings of worthlessness," "paranoid," "indecisiveness," "lacking coping skills," "suffering from mood swings," "trust issues," "crisis preoccupied," "unable to handle crises," "fear of being involved," "fear of rejection," "inability to believe in oneself," "problem understanding," "lack of self-confidence," "emotionally inflexible," "routinely violating confidentiality," "difficulty envisioning a future (self)," "tends to be very aggressive," "giving up too easily," "too sensitive," "not interested in what others feel," "likes to fix other people's problems," "talking too much and listening too little," "inappropriate responses or behavior," "problem adapting to various feelings," "lacks an enterprising spirit," "gets sad/depressed easily and often," "lacking purpose," "difficulty being alone," "antisocial," "usually quiet and withdrawn," "controlling," "self- centeredness," "too passive," "restless," "unhappy with choices made," "lacks leadership skills," "uncomfortable with oneself," "disinterested in being a good role model," "suffering from feelings of abandonment," "inability to control one's emotions," "emotionally distant," and so on. These are some of the dysfunctional behaviors that the sisters or nuns need to recognize and work on in order to experience happiness and fulfillment in their vocation.

As a way of refreshing our memories, we define dysfunctional behaviors as impaired functioning on the part of an individual person in any sort of relationship. The poor functioning refers to behaviors as well as relationships that are not working due to negative impacts. Behavioral issues like family conflicts, struggles with anxiety, and poverty are some of the issues that could change behavior. The nuns come from families to create a secondary family, the convent. By implication, they carry along both their strengths and weaknesses or dysfunctions.

Regular experience of conflict, misbehavior, or abuse in any way that causes disruptions in the convent, ender it dysfunctional.The sisters raised in such environments sometimes doubt themselves and their vocation. Some try to be manipulative and become sycophants to please their superiors; meanwhile, the superiors themselves might be unconsciously carrying on their own personal baggage of unresolved past family conflicts and undeveloped capacities.

In such a dysfunctional convent, the affected sisters do not stand up for themselves for fear of abandonment. At times, they would wish to belong to a different congregation or even get married. They blame others, not themselves, for their woes and project their anger and frustration on anyone who comes around them. Such a situation smacks of inauthentic living and stunted faith.

To address these dysfunctions, the researcher recommends that nuns and religious sisters undergo psychotherapy. This would help them resolve their past conflicts and fixations while at the same time helping them to develop the required capacities for mature religious life. It will also help them create their real and authentic selves. If the therapy goes well, the sister could stand to gain the following and more.

The **capacity to believe** enables one to be self-confident. It describes one with inner security. It is the ability to trust in others. In Erikson's psychosocial stages, the struggle is between **basic trust and basic mistrust**. Many sisters find trust to be elusive, leaving them with a serious sense of insecurity. As a result, they choose to protect themselves rather than let people know who they are. But since it is an unconscious act, they sometimes project a false sense of security to cover up. Both Erikson and Winnicott agree that a therapist, serving as a mother or caregiver, could work with sisters until their emotional and relational needs are taken care of or met. Consequently, the sisters would widen their social circles, thus striving toward independence. They would relate with others with a sense of trust, security, and hope, a capacity that would produce a sense of self-cohesiveness and confidence. It would enable the sisters to see one another as whole, independent, unique, and complete human beings imbued with dignity and worthy of respect.

With this achieved, the mature sister **develops the capacity to be alone in the presence of another**-the ability to contain her emotions and relate with others, which is linked to self-discovery and transformation of self. If a sister achieves the capacity to be alone in the presence of others, she is able to live creatively in the world as well as to contain the tension that living with others imposes. Since this capacity is related to emotional and spiritual maturity, the mature sister creates space for both her existence and that of others to live and discover what it means to live in turn. This agrees with Erikson's psychosocial stage of crisis between **initiative and guilt**, the successful resolution of which produces **purpose.**

With such a task achieved, the mature sister would feel free to relate with others with **the capacity to play**, which calls for spontaneity and creative engagement of others. In such an atmosphere, the nuns would play creatively even in their conversations. This would facilitate mental health improvement among the sisters and help them come alive. Since play comes from the inner space or self that feels secure, it is able to trust and take risks and be vulnerable. Playing together is a life-giving activity that enhances good relationships. Such an achievement would aid the sisters in moderating their emotions of anxiety as well as aggression. It would also help them to successfully work through Erikson's developmental stage of **intimacy versus isolation,** of which the end goal is **love.**

With this achievement, the mature sister would have **the capacity for concern** -the ability to manage her anger or destructiveness against others, and the courage and ability to be responsible for her own actions and then seek reparation when others are offended or hurt. Such behavior engenders the capacity to use others and be used. The latter capacity involves the ability to risk her vulnerability and allow others to be who they are. The mature nun would relate to people guided by emotional and relational forces full of authenticity, vulnerability, and intimacy. Such a nun would accept herself for who she is while also accepting others for who they are. This attitude would have a great positive impact on the sister's particular ministry and that of the congregation in general. Such a mature sister must have successfully resolved the psychosocial crisis between **generativity and stagnation**, of which the end goal, Erikson says, is **care.** "If these capacities are poorly developed, one can recognize that in the traits, behavior, and choices of a person" (Hamman 2014, 210). The same is obtained if there are fixations in any of Erikson's eight stages of growth and development. This is why the service of a good therapist is needed to help the sisters discover and transform their weaknesses into strength.

**Recommendations and Conclusions**

The following recommendations have been made based on the findings and the conclusions made.

Since religious women relate to all groups of people, it is proper for a sister to be in a position where she can create enough space for friends and the numerous people they encounter in their ministries. We are called to nurture our own space in order to be secure enough to carry out the various apostolates or ministries so as to be more productive. Achieving Winnicott's capacity to be alone is a very important stage for one who is seeking to be a religious sister. A religious sister lacking the capacity to be alone will make her ministry become like a desert. It is interesting to note how one can be alone when serving as a member of a religious community or in the presence of other religious sisters. Bonhoeffer writes, "Only in the community do we learn to be properly alone, ... and only in being alone... do we learn to live properly in the community" (1954, 83). This quote from Bonhoeffer reminds me of a song the sisters sing in one of their evening prayers:

*__Alone with None but Thee, My God__*
*Alone with none but thee, my God,*
*I journey on my way:*
*what need I fear when thou art near,*

*O King of night and day?*
*more safe am I within thy hand*
*than if a host should round me stand.*

*My destined time is known to thee,*
*and death will keep his hour;*
*did warriors strong around me throng,*
*they could not stay his power:*
*No walls of stone can man defend*
*when thou thy messenger dost send.*

*My life I yield to thy decree, and bow to thy control*
*in peaceful calm, for from thine arm*
*no power can wrest my soul:*
*could earthly omens e'er appal*
*a man that heeds the heavenly call?*

*The child of God can fear no ill,*
*his chosen, dread no foe;*
*we leave our fate with thee, and wait*
*thy bidding when to go:*
*'tis not from chance our comfort springs,*
*thou art our trust, O King of kings.*
*(ca. 1915, 521-597, trans. anonymous)*

For a religious sister, the aloneness or solitude with God gives her the opportunity, the capability, and the capacity to relate with others in community. On the idea of solitude, Nouwen writes,

*The solitude that really counts is the solitude of the heart; it is an inner quality or attitude that does not depend on physical isolation.... Solitude is one of the human capacities that can exist, be maintained and developed in the center of a big city, in the middle of a large crowd and in the context of a very active and productive life. A man or a woman who has developed this solitude of heart is no longer pulled apart by the most divergent stimuli of the surrounding world but is able to perceive and understand this world in a quiet innercenter. (1986, 37-38)*

Nurturing her core is also something the sister will need to do to minister effectively without feeling any stagnation (Erikson seventh stage of psychosocial development). Stagnant sisters are alive but dead religious women. Sometimes people think that merely having the desire to be a religious sister, to want to serve God, is enough. They likely have not thought about the community- living situation where they will encounter others.

The first thing that religious communities need to do is to come to terms with the fact that they have behavioral problems, from the superior general to the postulant. When this is acknowledged, it will be a bit easier for them to look at the problem in a more effective way. They could identify their past traumas, recognize where their behaviors are anchored, and learn a healthy way of relating.

Second, sisters need basic psychological courses or workshops on mother-infant relationships and how they affect growing children to assist all professed sisters in reconciling their childhood experiences and making sense of how those have impacted them in the present, especially in their decision-making processes. They would need to begin to understand and think about how their upbringing affected their attachment styles and work on breaking those patterns. It is paramount that the individual choosing to become a religious have a grasp on her inner life.

Third, the study shows that young ladies who choose to join the religious life do not know or understand their inner worlds and therefore need to be assisted through a psychological lens how to do this. They need to be educated to understand that insecure attachments trigger most often underlying interactions in the level of emotional arousal and reactivity. Each woman needs to ascertain whether she faces any inward impediments to the religious life and could undergo psychological testing to this end. Deliberate efforts need to be made to remove all circumstances and impediments that could frustrate those who choose to join and who have healthy personalities.

Additionally, those in formation (temporal, novices, and postulants) need to be assisted through exposure to basic psychological courses to help identify past traumas, recognize where their behaviors are anchored, and move forward with a more positive self-view, which in turn will help them form healthy and secure attachments affecting their dealings with others.

Finally, with the researcher's experience as a psychoanalyst for more than ten years and a religious sister for more than thirty years, she has the capacity to make this case and has attempted to do this as objectively as possible. Since religious life is a calling (voluntary choice), people will feel compelled to respond, but the need for an interior attitude of trust and openness is important. It is a personal choice, and one ought to "find his or her own self and feel real. Feeling real is more than existing; it is finding a way to exist as oneself and to relate to objects as oneself and to have a self into which to retreat for relaxation" (Winnicott 2005, 158).

# Works Cited

Achebe, C. 1958. *Things Fall Apart.* Oxford:
  Heinemann Educational Publishers.
Adams, M. V. 1996. *The Multicultural Imagination*:
  *"Race," Color and the Unconscious.* New York: Routledge.
Ainsworth, M. D., M. C. Blehar, E. Waters, and S. Wall. 1978.
  *Pattern of Attachmen*: A Psychoanalytical Study of the
Strange  Situation. Hillsdale, NJ: Lawrence Erlbaum Associates.
Akhtar, S. 2009a. Comprehensive Dictionary of Psychoanalysis.
  London: Karnac Books.
Akhtar, S. 2009b. *Good Feelings*:
  *Psychoanalytical Reflections on Positive*
  *Creation and Attitudes.* London: Karnac Books.
Allport, F. H. 1995. *Theories of Perception and*
  Concept of Structures. New York: John Willey & Son Inc.
Allport, G. W. 1955. *Becoming: Basic*
  *Consideration for a Psychology of Personality.*
  London: Yale University Press.
______.1961. *Pattern and Growth in*
  *Personality.* New York: H. Rinehard.
______.1937. Personality: A Psychological I
  *Interpretation.* New York: H. Holt and
  Company.
Altman, N. 1995. The Analyst in the Inner
  *City: Race, Color, Class, and Culture, through*
  *a Psychoanalytical Lens.* New Jersey: The
  Analytic Press.
American Behavioral Clinics.
  "Psychological Maturity." http://
  americanbehavioralclinic.com
*The American Heritage Collegiate Dictionary*,
  3rd ed. 1993. Boston, New York: Houghton
  Mifflin Company, p. 1,019.
American Psychiatric Association. 2013. *Desk*

*Reference to the Diagnostic Criteria form* DSM
5. Washington, DC: American Psychiatric
Publishing.

Anderson, C. L. 2008. *Drowning in My Mother's
Womb.* New York: Loyola Publishing.

APA *Dictionary of Psychology.* 2006.
Washington, DC: American Psychological
Association.

Augustine, S. 1955. *Confessions.* Philadelphia:
The Westminster Press.

Babbie, H. S. 1990. *Survey Research Methods,*
2nd ed. New Delhi: Practice Hall of India
Private Ltd.

Barnard, K. E. 1982. Reported in F. A.
Pederson, "Father Influences Viewed in a
Family Context." In M. E. Lamb (ed). *The Role
of the Father in the Child Development,* 2nd ed.
New York: John Wiley.

Bartley, H. S. 1969. Principles of Perception, 2nd
ed. New York: Harper & Row Publishers.

Basch, M. F. 1980. Doing Psychotherapy. New
York: Basic Books.

Berryman, J. W. 1991. Godly Play: A Way
*of Religious Education.* San Francisco:
HarperSanFrancisco.

Bollas, C. 1989. *The Shadow of the Object.* New
York: Columbia University Press.

Bonhoeffer, D. 1954. Life Together. New York:
Harper & Row.

Bowlby, J______. (1969) 1982. *Attachment
and Loss,* Vol. 1. New York: Basic Books.

______.1973. *Separation: Anxiety and Anger.*
New York: Basic Books.

______. 1973. *Separation: Anxiety and Anger,*
Vol. 2: Attachment and Loss. New York: Basic Books.

______.1980. Loss: *Sadness and Depression.*
New York: Basic Books.

______. 1988. *A Secure Base: Parent-
Child Attachment and Healthy Human*

Development. London: Routledge.

______.2006. *The Making and Breaking of Affectional Bonds* (reprint). London: Routledge.

Bradshaw, J. 2005. *Healing the Shame that Binds You*. Florida: Health Communications.

Bradshaw, J. 1990. *Home Coming: Reclaiming and Championing Your Inner Child*. New York: Banton Books.

Brazelton, T. B., and B. G. Cramer. 1990. *The Earliest Relationships: Parents, Infants, and the Early Drama of Early Attachments*. Reading, MA: Perseus Books.

Brenner, I. 2001. *Dissociation of Trauma: Theory, Phenomenology and Technique*. Madison, CT: International University Press.

Bruner, J. S., J. J. Goodnow, and G. A. Austin. 1956. A Study of Thinking. New York: Longman.

Cameron, N. 1963. *Personality Development and Psychopathology: A Dynamic Approach*. Boston: Houghton Mifflin Company.

"Catholic Vocation Discernment." Paths of Love. http://www.pathsoflove.com

Chapman, G., and R. Campbell. 2005. *The Five Love Languages of Children*. Chicago: Northfield Publishing.

Cherry, K. December 7, 2009. *Identity vs. Role Confusion in Psychosocial Stage 5*. Very Well Mind. http://www.verywellmind.com/psychosocialpsychology.

Clinebell, H. 1995. Counseling for Spiritually *Empowered Wholeness: A Hope Centered Approach*. Binghamton, NY: The Haworth Pastoral Press.

Colarusso, C. 1992. *Child and Adult*

*Development.* New York: Plenum.

Coles, Robert. 2000. *The Erik Erikson Reader.* New York: W.W. Norton & Company.

Cori, J. L. 2010. *The Emotionally Absent Mother,* 2nd ed. New York: The Experiment.

Dummies.com. "Rosary beads." Updated March 15, 2022. https:// www.dummies.com.

Encyclopaedia Britannica Online, Academic ed. s.v. "catechumen." Edited July 29, 2013. https://www.britannica.com/topic/ catechumen.

Erikson, E. 1963. *Childhood and Society.* New York: W. W. Norton and Company.

_____.1966. *The Concept of Identity in Race Relations,* American Academy of Arts and Sciences Archives, ERIC ED012730.

_____.1968. *Identity: Youth and Crisis.* New York: W. W. Norton Company.

_____.1980. *Identity and the Life Cycle.* New York: W. W. Norton Company.

_____.1997. *The Life Cycle Completed.* New York: W. W. Norton Company.

Evans, R. I. 1967. Dialogue with Erik Erikson. New York: Harper & Row.

Fairbairn, W. R. D. 1952b. Psycho-Analytic *Studies of the Personality.* London: Tavistock Publications Ltd.

_____. 1992. *Psychoanalytic Studies of the Personality.* New York: Routledge.

_____.1994. *From Instinct to Self: Selected Papers of W. R. D. Fairbairn.* Vol. 1. Edited by David E. Scharff and Ellinor Fairbairn Birtles. NJ: Jason Aronson Inc.

Feist, J., and G. J. Feist. 2009. *Theories of Personality,* 7th ed. New York: McGraw Hill.

Forward, S. 2014. *Mothers Who Can't Love: A Healing Guide for Daughters.* New York:

HarperCollins Publications.

Fraiberg, S. H. 1996. *The Magic Years: Understanding and Handling the Problems of Early Childhood.* New York: Macmillan Publishing Company.

Franz, M. L.V. 1996. *The Interpretation of Fairy Tales.* Boston: Shambhala.

Fromm, E. 2001. *The Fear of Freedom.* London: Routledge & Kegan Paul.

Gay, P. 1987. *Freud: A Life for Our Time.* New York Norton.

Global Sisters Report. "Final professed." Updated July 4, 2022. https://www.globalsistersreport.org.

Greenberg, J. R., and S. A. Mitchell. 1983. *Object Relations in Psychoanalytic Theory,* 1st ed. Cambridge, MA: Harvard University Press.

Guntrip, H. 1956. *Mental Pain and Care of Souls.* London: Independent Press.

______.1969. *Schizoid Phenomena, Object Relations and the Self.* Madison, CT: International University Press.

Hamaker-Zondag, Karen. 2018. *Carl Jung and Astrology in Psychoanalysis.* City: Publisher. Online.

Hamman, J. J. 2014. *Becoming a Pastor: Forming Self and Soul for Ministry.* Cleveland, OH: The Pilgrim Press.

Harbaugh, G. L. 1984.*Pastor as a Person: Maintaining Personal Integrity in the Choices and Challenges of Ministry.* Minneapolis: Augsbury Publishing House.

Hartman, D., and D. Zimberoff. 2009. "The Hero's Journey of Self-Transformation: Models of Higher Development from Mythology.*" Journal of Heart-Centered Therapies* 12(2), pp. 3-93.

Herman, J. 1997. *Trauma and Recovery: The*

*Aftermath of Violence-from Domestic Abuse to Political Terror*. New York: Basic Books.

Hesse, H. 1968. *The Journey to the East*. New York: The Noonday Press.

Holland, S. L. (ed.). 1985. *The Code of Canon Law: Institute of Consecrated Life*. Edited by J. A. Corriden, T. G. Green, and D. E. Heintschel. New York: Paulist Press, p. 454. The Holy See. n.d. Vatican website. https://www.vatican.va

Hopkins, B. 1977. "Winnicott and the Capacity to Believe." *International Journal of Psychoanalysis, 78*.

Huston, J. P., C. Hammen, A. Padilla, and H. Bee. 1989. Invitation to Psychology, 3rd ed. New York: Harcourt Brace, Jovanovich Publishers.

Jacobus, M. 2006. *The Poetics of Psychoanalysis. In The Wake of Klein*. Oxford: Oxford University Press.

James, W. 2009. *The Varieties of Religious Experience: A Study in Human Nature.* New York: Seven Treasures Publications.

*The Jerusalem Bible*. 1966. London: Eyre & Spottiswoode.

Jung, C. G. 1954. *The Practice of Psychotherapy.* Princeton: Bollingen Series.

Kalsched, D. 1996. *The Inner World of Trauma: Archetypal Defense of the Personal Spirit.* New York: Routledge.

Kast, V. 1997. *Father Daughter Mother Son.* Great Britain: Element Books Limited.

Mahler, M. 1972. "On the First Three Subphases of the Separation-Individuation Process." *The International Journal of Psychoanalysis* 53, pp. 333-337.

______.1972. "On Child Psychosis and Schizophrenia: Autistic and Symbiotic." *The*

*Psychoanalytic Study of the Child*, 7(1).

______.1994. "Symbiosis and Individuation: The Psychological Birth of the Human Infant." *The Separation Individuation*. New York: Rowman & Littlefield Publishers, Inc.

Malcolm, J. 1988. *Psychoanalysis*: The *Impossible Profession*. London, New York:

Mahler, M., F. Pine., and A. Berman. 1975. *The Psychological Birth of the Human Infant*. New York: Basic Books.

Maslow, A. H. 1970. *Motivation and Personality*, 2nd ed. New York: Harper & Row.

______.1970. *Religions, Values and Peak Experiences*. Menlo Park, CA: The W. P. Laughlin Charitable Foundation.

May, R. 1981. *Man's Search for Himself*. New York: W.W. Norton & Company, Inc.

McNish, J. L. 2004. *Transforming Shame: A Pastoral Response*. Binghamton, NY: Haworth Pastoral Press.

McWilliams, N. 1994. *Psychoanalytic Diagnosis: Understanding Personality Structure in the Clinical Process*. New York: The Guilford Press.

Merriam-Webster Online Dictionary. S.v. "postulancy." Accessed DATE. URL

Miller, A. 1998. *Thou Shall Not Be Aware*. New York: Farrar Straus Giroux.

______.2004a. *The Drama of Being a Child*. *New York:* Farrar Straus Giroux.

______.2004b. *The Drama of the Gifted Child*. New York: Farrar Straus Giroux.

Minsky, R. 2006. *Psychanalysis and Gender*. London: Psychology Press.

Muuss, R. E. 1962. *Theories of Adolescence*, 6th ed. New York: McGraw Hill Companies.

Neumann, E. 1988. *The Child: Structure*

*and Dynamic of the Nascent Personality.* H. Karnac.

New Advent. "Postulancy." Accessed DATE. https://www.newadvent.org.

Nicholas, M. P. 2004. *Family Therapy: Concept and Method.* New York: Pearson Education Inc..

Nouwen, H. J. M. 1986. *Reaching Out: The Three Movements of the Spiritual Life.* Garden City: Image Books.

Ogden, T. H. 2004. "On Holding and Containing: Being and Dreaming." *International Journal of Psychoanalysis* 85, 1349-1364.

Otto, R. 2010. *The Idea of the Holy: An Inquiry into the Non-rational Factor in the Idea of the Divine and Its Relation to the Rational.* Mansfield Center, CT: Martino Publishing.

Pargament, K. 2011. *Spiritually Integrated Psychotherapy: Understanding and Addressing the Sacred.* New York: The Guilford Press.

Peck, M. S. 2003. *The Road Less Travelled: A New Psychology of Love, Traditional Values and Spiritual Growth.* New York: Simon & Schuster.

Perfectae Caritatis (of perfect charity) 1985. Decree of the adaptation and renewal of religious life, issued by the second Vatican Council (1965) canons (573-730) which deals specifically with institutes of consecrated life in the catholic church. The code of canon law: a text and commentary, by Sharon L. Holland: New York, Paulist Press.

Person, E. S., A. M. Copper, and G. O. Gabbard. 2005. *Textbook of Psychoanalysis.* Washington, DC: The American Psychiatric Publishing Inc.

Rogers, C. R. 1967. *On Becoming a Person: A Therapist's View of Psychotherapy.* London: Constable & Company Ltd.

Rothschild, B. 2000. *The Body Remembers: The Psychophysiology of Trauma Treatment.* New York: Norton & Company.

Royal College of Psychiatrists. "Spirituality." Accessed 2022. https://www.rcpsych.ac.uk

Scharff, J., and D. Scharff. 1997. *The Primer of Object Relations* Theory. Northvale, New Jersey: Jarson Aronson Inc.

Stern, D. 1985. *The Interpersonal World of the Infant: A View from Psychoanalysis and Developmental Psychology.* New York: Basic Books.

______.1998. *The Motherhood Constellation.* London: Karnac Books.

Tagiuri, R., and L. Petrullo. 1958. *Person Perception and Interpersonal Behavior.* Stanford, CA: Stanford University.

Tillich, P. 1984. *Meaning of Health: Essays in Existentialism, Psychoanalysis, and Religion.* Chicago: Exploration Press.

Titus, H. H., S. M. Smith, and T. T. Nolan. 1979. *Living Issues in Philosophy,* 7th ed. New York: D. Van Nostrand Company.

Walton, J. 1969. *Administration and Policy Making in Education,* rev. ed. Baltimore: Johns Hopkins Press.

Whitman, Walt. 2007 (reprint*), Leaves of Grass.* Mineola, NY: Dover Publishing Inc.

Wikipedia. s.v. "diocesan rights." Accessed 2021. https://en.m.wikipedia.org/wiki/Diocesan_rights.

______. s.v. "novitiatea." Accessed 2021. https://en.wikipedia.org/wiki/novitiatea

______.s.v. "pontifical rights." Accessed 2021 https://en.wikipedia.org/wiki/

pontifical_rights
______.s.v. "religious sister." Accessed 2021. URL

______.s.v. "religious vows." Accessed 2021. URL

______.s.v. "SOS." Accessed 2021. URL

______.s.v. "temporal professed." Accessed 2021. URL

Winnicott, D. W. 1956. "Primary Maternal Preoccupation." In *Through Pediatrics to Psychoanalysis*. New York: Basic Books.

______.1958. "Primary Maternal Preoccupation." In *Through Pediatrics to Psychoanalysis: Collected Papers.* London: Tavistock.

______. 1958. "Aggression and Its Relation to EmotionalDevelopment." In *Through Pediatrics to Psychoanalysis: Collected Papers.* London: Tavistock.

______.1960. "Ego Distortion in Terms of True and False Self." *The Maturational Process and the Facilitating Environment: Studies in the Theory of Emotional Development.* New York: International Universities Press, Inc.

______.1960. "The Theory of the Parent-Infant Relationship." In *The Maturational Process and the Facilitating Environment.* London & New York: Karnac, 1960.

______.1962. "Ego Integration in Child Development." In *The Maturational Process and the Facilitating Environment.* London & New York: Karnac, 1962.

______.1963. "Capacity for Concern." In *Maturational Process and the Facilitating Environment.* London: Karnac Books.

______1964. *The Child, the Family, and the Outside World. New* York: Addison-Wesley Publishing Company, Inc.

______.1971. "Mirror Role of Mother and

Family in Child Development." *In Playing and Reality*. New York: Brunner-Routledge.

______.1971. "The Transitional Objects and Transitional Phenomena." *In Playing and Reality*. New York: Brunner-Routledge.

______.1971. "The Use of Objects and Relating through Identification*." In Playing and Reality*. New York: Brunner-Routledge.

______.1989. *Psychoanalytic Exploration*. Cambridge, MA: Harvard University Press.

______.1990. "From Dependence Towards Independence." In *The Maturational Process and the Facilitating Environment* (Ch. 7). London & New York: Karnac.

______.1990. *The Maturational Process and the Facilitating Environment*. London: Karnac Books.

______.2005. *Playing and Reality*. London: Routledge.

Winnicott, D. W., R. Shepherd, and M. Davis, eds. 1986. *Home Is Where We Start From: Essays by a Psychoanalyst*. New York: W. W. Norton and Company.

Wright, H. N. 2001. *The Complete Guide to Crisis and Trauma Counseling*. CITY CA: Regal.

Wundt, W. 1904. *Principles of Physiological Psychology,* 5th ed. New York: Macmillan.

Yalom, I. D. 1995. *The Theory and Practice of Group Psychotherapy*, 4th ed. New York: Basic Books.

https://Vatican.va/roman_curia/ congregations/ccscrlife/document.rc

*Appendix*

# Questionnaire

Dear Participant, thank you for your participation in this study. I appreciate your time and effort in doing this. This questionnaire is a part of my research studies. It is about what makes for a good Religious Sister (Nun). Please answer all the questions as fully as you can and return the questionnaire to the person from whom you received it. Thank you again and God bless you.

**Years you have been in the congregation**

**Level in the congregation: Final Professed**

**Temporal Professed Novitiate Postulancy**

1. Did you grow up with your father? (circle one) Y N If yes respond continue to the next question (if No skip the next question).

2. Indicate which things you hadexperienced in the relationship you had with your father: My father supported and encouraged me to become a leader.

My father was a positive role model for me.

My father was affectionate and playful with me.

My father spent time listening to me and having conversation with me.

My father would show up at my school and community activities and performances.

My father encouraged me to do good at  whatever I was doing.

My father publicly rebuked or shamed me when I made mistakes.

My father punished me when I made mistakes.

My father encouraged me to do better when I made mistakes or fell short.

My father prevented or discouraged me from doing or pursuing things I liked. My father was present in the home but did not interact positively with me.

My father drove fear into me.

My father did not show me that he loved me.

My father tried to control what I did and how I did it.

My father made me feel inadequate or not good enough.

___________ My father physically abused me.

Thank you for completing this questionnaire. Below you will find **seven columns**; the **first column** has a list of behaviors. In the **second column** indicate with a **"X"** those behaviors you observed among all the sisters in your congregation. In **the third column**, indicate with an **"F"** those behaviors you observed among sisters who made their final vows; in the **fourth column** indicate with a **"T"** those behaviors you observed among sisters who have made temporal vows; in the **fifth column** indicate with a **"p"** those behaviors you observed among postulants; in the **sixth column**, please indicate with a **"N"** those behaviors you observed among novitiates; in the **seventh column** indicate with an **"M"** those behaviors that you observed in yourself. Thanks again for your patience and help in completing this research project.

| | Behaviors you observed among the sisters in your congregation (X) | Behaviors you observed in Sisters who made Final vows (F) | Behaviors in sisters who made temporal vows (T) | Behaviors observed in postulants Sisters (P) | Behaviors observed in novitiates (N) | Your behaviors (M) |
|---|---|---|---|---|---|---|
| Untrusting | | | | | | |
| Difficulty making and keeping friends | | | | | | |
| Tend to be angry most of the time | | | | | | |
| Tends to be needy | | | | | | |
| Tends to be overly defensive | | | | | | |
| Tends to be very aggressive | | | | | | |
| Recognition seeking | | | | | | |
| Self-blaming | | | | | | |
| Anxious | | | | | | |
| Low self-esteem | | | | | | |
| Feelings of being ridiculed | | | | | | |
| Emotionally distant or unavailable | | | | | | |
| Tend to get into other people stuff | | | | | | |
| Discipline or retaliating by shaming | | | | | | |
| Feelings of loneliness | | | | | | |
| Fear of being judged | | | | | | |
| Feelings of worthlessness | | | | | | |
| Paranoid | | | | | | |
| Indecisive | | | | | | |
| Lacking coping skills | | | | | | |
| Suffer from mood swings | | | | | | |
| Trust issues | | | | | | |
| Crisis preoccupied | | | | | | |
| Unable to handle crisis | | | | | | |
| Fear of getting involved | | | | | | |
| Fear of rejection | | | | | | |
| Does not believe in oneself | | | | | | |
| Problems understanding | | | | | | |
| Lacking self-confidence | | | | | | |
| Emotionally inflexible | | | | | | |
| Routinely violates confidentiality | | | | | | |
| Difficulty envisioning a future (self) | | | | | | |

| | | | | | |
|---|---|---|---|---|---|
| Gives up easily | | | | | |
| Too sensitive | | | | | |
| Not interested in what others feel | | | | | |
| Likes to fix other people's problems | | | | | |
| Talks too much and listens too little | | | | | |
| Inappropriate responses or behavior | | | | | |
| Problems adapting to various feelings | | | | | |
| Lacks the enterprising spirit | | | | | |
| Gets sad/depressed easily and often | | | | | |
| Lacking purpose | | | | | |
| Difficulty being alone | | | | | |
| Antisocial | | | | | |
| Usually quiet and withdrawn | | | | | |
| Controlling | | | | | |
| Self-centeredness | | | | | |
| Too passive | | | | | |
| Restless | | | | | |
| Unhappy with choices made | | | | | |
| Uncomfortable with oneself | | | | | |
| Lacks leadership skills | | | | | |
| Disinterest in being a good role model | | | | | |
| Suffers from feelings of abandonment | | | | | |
| Inability to control one's emotions | | | | | |

# *About the Author*

**Patience Quayson,** a native of Ghana, West Africa, attended Catholic school and sang in her local church choir. She has been a religious sister for more than thirty years, serving as the vocation director of her order for more than twenty years. In 1986, she was sent to Rome to study, graduating with a master's in theology. In the year 2000 she graduated from Cape Coast University, Ghana with masters in Educational Administration. Later, she earned a Doctor of Ministry and a Ph.D. in pastoral psychology. A licensed psychoanalyst, she is a psychoanalyst/ psychotherapist at Blanton Peale, Manhattan, New York.